The Pelican Shakespeare
General Editors

STEPHEN ORGEL
A. R. BRAUNMULLER

All's Well That Ends Well

An eighteenth-century Helena: Maria Macklin (1733-1781),
daughter of Charles Macklin, the most famous Shylock of the
age. Maria Macklin first played Helena in 1756, and though not
a great success, appeared regularly at Drury Lane throughout
her career. She was most praised in trouser roles.
From Bell's Shakespeare, 1776.

William Shakespeare

———

All's Well That Ends Well

EDITED BY CLAIRE MCEACHERN

PENGUIN BOOKS

PENGUIN BOOKS
Published by the Penguin Group
Penguin Putnam Inc., 375 Hudson Street,
New York, New York 10014, U.S.A.
Penguin Books Ltd, 27 Wrights Lane,
London W8 5TZ, England
Penguin Books Australia Ltd, Ringwood,
Victoria, Australia
Penguin Books Canada Ltd, 10 Alcorn Avenue,
Toronto, Ontario, Canada M4V 3B2
Penguin Books (N.Z.) Ltd, 182–190 Wairau Road,
Auckland 10, New Zealand

Penguin Books Ltd, Registered Offices:
Harmondsworth, Middlesex, England

All's Well That Ends Well edited by Jonas A. Barish published in
the United States of America in Penguin Books 1964
Revised edition published 1980
This new edition edited by Claire McEachern published 2001

1   3   5   7   9   10   8   6   4   2

LIBRARY OF CONGRESS CATALOGING IN PUBLICATION DATA
Shakespeare, William, 1564–1616.
All's well that ends well / William Shakespeare ;
edited by Claire McEachern.
p.   cm. – (The Pelican Shakespeare)
ISBN 0 14 07.1460 -X (pbk. : alk. paper)
1. Florence (Italy) – Drama.   2. Runaway husbands – Drama.
3. Married women – Drama.
I. McEachern, Claire Elizabeth, 1963–   II. Title.   III. Series.
PR2801.A2 M38 2001
822.3'3 – dc21   2001031341

Printed in the United States of America
Set in Adobe Garamond
Designed by Virginia Norey

Contents

Publisher's Note

IT IS ALMOST half a century since the first volumes of the Pelican Shakespeare appeared under the general editorship of Alfred Harbage. The fact that a new edition, rather than simply a revision, has been undertaken reflects the profound changes textual and critical studies of Shakespeare have undergone in the past twenty years. For the new Pelican series, the texts of the plays and poems have been thoroughly revised in accordance with recent scholarship, and in some cases have been entirely reedited. New introductions and notes have been provided in all the volumes. But the new Shakespeare is also designed as a successor to the original series; the previous editions have been taken into account, and the advice of the previous editors has been solicited where it was feasible to do so.

Certain textual features of the new Pelican Shakespeare should be particularly noted. All lines are numbered that contain a word, phrase, or allusion explained in the glossarial notes. In addition, for convenience, every tenth line is also numbered, in italics when no annotation is indicated. The intrusive and often inaccurate place headings inserted by early editors are omitted (as is becoming standard practice), but for the convenience of those who miss them, an indication of locale now appears as the first item in the annotation of each scene.

In the interest of both elegance and utility, each speech prefix is set in a separate line when the speaker's lines are in verse, except when those words form the second half of a verse line. Thus the verse form of the speech is kept visually intact. What is printed as verse and what is printed as prose has, in general, the authority of the original texts. Departures from the original texts in this regard have only the authority of editorial tradition and the judgment of the Pelican editors; and, in a few instances, are admittedly arbitrary.

The Theatrical World

ECONOMIC REALITIES determined the theatrical world in which Shakespeare's plays were written, performed, and received. For centuries in England, the primary theatrical tradition was nonprofessional. Craft guilds (or "mysteries") provided religious drama – mystery plays – as part of the celebration of religious and civic festivals, and schools and universities staged classical and neoclassical drama in both Latin and English as part of their curricula. In these forms, drama was established and socially acceptable. Professional theater, in contrast, existed on the margins of society. The acting companies were itinerant; playhouses could be any available space – the great halls of the aristocracy, town squares, civic halls, inn yards, fair booths, or open fields – and income was sporadic, dependent on the passing of the hat or on the bounty of local patrons. The actors, moreover, were considered little better than vagabonds, constantly in danger of arrest or expulsion.

In the late 1560s and 1570s, however, English professional theater began to gain respectability. Wealthy aristocrats fond of drama – the Lord Admiral, for example, or the Lord Chamberlain – took acting companies under their protection so that the players technically became members of their households and were no longer subject to arrest as homeless or masterless men. Permanent theaters were first built at this time as well, allowing the companies to control and charge for entry to their performances.

Shakespeare's livelihood, and the stunning artistic explosion in which he participated, depended on pragmatic and architectural effort. Professional theater requires ways to restrict access to its offerings; if it does not, and admission fees cannot be charged, the actors do not get paid, the costumes go to a pawnbroker, and there is no such thing as a professional, ongoing theatrical tradition. The answer to that economic need arrived in the late 1560s and 1570s with the creation of the so-called public or amphitheater playhouse. Recent discoveries indicate that the precursor of the Globe playhouse in London (where Shakespeare's mature plays were presented) and the Rose theater (which presented Christopher Marlowe's plays and some of Shakespeare's earliest ones) was the Red Lion theater of 1567. Archaeological studies of the foundations of the Rose and Globe theaters have revealed that the open-air theater of the 1590s and later was probably a polygonal building with fourteen to twenty or twenty-four sides, multistoried, from 75 to 100 feet in diameter, with a raised, partly covered "thrust" stage that projected into a group of standing patrons, or "groundlings," and a covered gallery, seating up to 2,500 or more (very crowded) spectators.

These theaters might have been about half full on any given day, though the audiences were larger on holidays or when a play was advertised, as old and new were, through printed playbills posted around London. The metropolitan area's late-Tudor, early-Stuart population (circa 1590-1620) has been estimated at about 150,000 to 250,000. It has been supposed that in the mid-1590s there were about 15,000 spectators per week at the public theaters; thus, as many as 10 percent of the local population went to the theater regularly. Consequently, the theaters' repertories – the plays available for this experienced and frequent audience – had to change often: in the month between September 15 and October 15, 1595, for instance, the Lord Admiral's Men performed twenty-eight times in eighteen different plays.

Since natural light illuminated the amphitheaters' stages, performances began between noon and two o'clock and ran without a break for two or three hours. They often concluded with a jig, a fencing display, or some other nondramatic exhibition. Weather conditions determined the season for the amphitheaters: plays were performed every day (including Sundays, sometimes, to clerical dismay) except during Lent – the forty days before Easter – or periods of plague, or sometimes during the summer months when law courts were not in session and the most affluent members of the audience were not in London.

To a modern theatergoer, an amphitheater stage like that of the Rose or Globe would appear an unfamiliar mixture of plainness and elaborate decoration. Much of the structure was carved or painted, sometimes to imitate marble; elsewhere, as under the canopy projecting over the stage, to represent the stars and the zodiac. Appropriate painted canvas pictures (of Jerusalem, for example, if the play was set in that city) were apparently hung on the wall behind the acting area, and tragedies were accompanied by black hangings, presumably something like crepe festoons or bunting. Although these theaters did not employ what we would call scenery, early modern spectators saw numerous large props, such as the "bar" at which a prisoner stood during a trial, the "mossy bank" where lovers reclined, an arbor for amorous conversation, a chariot, gallows, tables, trees, beds, thrones, writing desks, and so forth. Audiences might learn a scene's location from a sign (reading "Athens," for example) carried across the stage (as in Bertolt Brecht's twentieth-century productions). Equally captivating (and equally irritating to the theater's enemies) were the rich costumes and personal props the actors used: the most valuable items in the surviving theatrical inventories are the swords, gowns, robes, crowns, and other items worn or carried by the performers.

Magic appealed to Shakespeare's audiences as much as it does to us today, and the theater exploited many deceptive and spectacular devices. A winch in the loft above the stage, called "the heavens," could lower and raise actors playing gods, goddesses, and other supernatural figures to and from the main acting area, just as one or more trapdoors permitted entrances and exits to and from the area, called "hell," beneath the stage. Actors wore elementary makeup such as wigs, false beards, and face paint, and they employed pig's bladders filled with animal blood to make wounds seem more real. They had rudimentary but effective ways of pretending to behead or hang a person. Supernumeraries (stagehands or actors not needed in a particular scene) could make thunder sounds (by shaking a metal sheet or rolling an iron ball down a chute) and show lightning (by blowing inflammable resin through tubes into a flame). Elaborate fireworks enhanced the effects of dragons flying through the air or imitated such celestial phenomena as comets, shooting stars, and multiple suns. Horses' hoofbeats, bells (located perhaps in the tower above the stage), trumpets and drums, clocks, cannon shots and gunshots, and the like were common sound effects. And the music of viols, cornets, oboes, and recorders was a regular feature of theatrical performances.

For two relatively brief spans, from the late 1570s to 1590 and from 1599 to 1614, the amphitheaters competed with the so-called private, or indoor, theaters, which originated as, or later represented themselves as, educational institutions training boys as singers for church services and court performances. These indoor theaters had two features that were distinct from the amphitheaters': their personnel and their playing spaces. The amphitheaters' adult companies included both adult men, who played the male roles, and boys, who played the female roles; the private, or indoor, theater companies, on the other hand, were entirely composed of boys aged about 8 to 16, who were, or could pretend to be, candidates for singers in a church or a royal boys' choir. (Until 1660, professional theatrical companies included no women.) The playing space would appear much more familiar to modern audiences than the long-vanished amphitheaters; the later indoor theaters were, in fact, the ancestors of the typical modern theater. They were enclosed spaces, usually rectangular, with the stage filling one end of the rectangle and the audience arrayed in seats or benches across (and sometimes lining) the building's longer axis. These spaces staged plays less frequently than the public theaters (perhaps only once a week) and held far fewer spectators than the amphitheaters: about 200 to 600, as opposed to 2,500 or more. Fewer patrons mean a smaller gross income, unless each pays more. Not surprisingly, then, private theaters charged higher prices than the amphitheaters, probably sixpence, as opposed to a penny for the cheapest entry.

Protected from the weather, the indoor theaters presented plays later in the day than the amphitheaters, and used artificial illumination – candles in sconces or candelabra. But candles melt, and need replacing, snuffing, and trimming, and these practical requirements may have been part of the reason the indoor theaters introduced breaks in the performance, the intermission so dear to the heart of theatergoers and to the pocketbooks of theater concessionaires ever since. Whether motivated by the need to tend to the candles or by the entrepreneurs' wishing to sell oranges and liquor, or both, the indoor theaters eventually established the modern convention of the non-continuous performance. In the early modern "private" theater, musical performances apparently filled the intermissions, which in Stuart theater jargon seem to have been called "acts."

At the end of the first decade of the seventeenth century, the distinction between public amphitheaters and private indoor companies ceased. For various cultural, political, and economic reasons, individual companies gained control of both the public, open-air theaters and the indoor ones, and companies mixing adult men and boys took over the formerly "private" theaters. Despite the death of the boys' companies and of their highly innovative theaters (for which such luminous playwrights as Ben Jonson, George Chapman, and John Marston wrote), their playing spaces and conventions had an immense impact on subsequent plays: not merely for the intervals (which stressed the artistic and architectonic importance of "acts"), but also because they introduced political and social satire as a popular dramatic ingredient, even in tragedy, and a wider range of actorly effects, encouraged by their more intimate playing spaces.

Even the briefest sketch of the Shakespearean theatrical world would be incomplete without some comment on the social and cultural dimensions of theaters and playing in the period. In an intensely hierarchical and status-conscious society, professional actors and their ventures had hardly any respectability; as we have indicated, to protect themselves against laws designed to curb vagabondage and the increase of masterless men, actors resorted to the near-fiction that they were the servants of noble masters, and wore their distinctive livery. Hence the company for which Shakespeare wrote in the 1590s called itself the Lord Chamberlain's Men and pretended that the public, money-getting performances were in fact rehearsals for private performances before that high court official. From 1598, the Privy Council had licensed theatrical companies, and after 1603, with the accession of King James I, the companies gained explicit royal protection, just as the Queen's Men had for a time under Queen Elizabeth. The Chamberlain's Men became the King's Men, and the other companies were patronized by the other members of the royal family.

These designations were legal fictions that half-concealed an important economic and social develop-ment, the evolution away from the theater's organization on the model of the guild, a self-regulating confraternity of individual artisans, into a proto-capitalist organization. Shakespeare's company became a joint-stock company, where persons who supplied capital and, in some cases, such as Shakespeare's, capital and talent, employed them-selves and others in earning a return on that capital. This development meant that actors and theater companies were outside both the traditional guild structures, which required some form of civic or royal charter, and the feu-dal household organization of master-and-servant. This anomalous, maverick social and economic condition

made theater companies practically unruly and potentially even dangerous; consequently, numerous official
bodies – including the London metropolitan and ecclesi-
astical authorities as well as, occasionally, the royal court
itself – tried, without much success, to control and even
to disband them.

Public officials had good reason to want to close the
theaters: they were attractive nuisances – they drew often
riotous crowds, they were always noisy, and they could be
politically offensive and socially insubordinate. Until the
Civil War, however, anti-theatrical forces failed to shut
down professional theater, for many reasons – limited
surveillance and few police powers, tensions or outright
hostilities among the agencies that sought to check or
channel theatrical activity, and lack of clear policies for
control. Another reason must have been the theaters' un-
deniable popularity. Curtailing any activity enjoyed by
such a substantial percentage of the population was diffi-
cult, as various Roman emperors attempting to limit cir-
cuses had learned, and the Tudor-Stuart audience was not
merely large, it was socially diverse and included women.
The prevalence of public entertainment in this period
has been underestimated. In fact, fairs, holidays, games,
sporting events, the equivalent of modern parades, freak
shows, and street exhibitions all abounded, but the theater was the most widely and frequently available entertainment to which people of every class had access. That
fact helps account both for its quantity and for the fear
and anger it aroused.

WILLIAM SHAKESPEARE OF
STRATFORD-UPON-AVON, GENTLEMAN

Many people have said that we know very little about
William Shakespeare's life – pinheads and postcards are
often mentioned as appropriately tiny surfaces on which
to record the available information. More imaginatively

and perhaps more correctly, Ralph Waldo Emerson wrote, "Shakespeare is the only biographer of Shakespeare. . . . So far from Shakespeare's being the least known, he is the one person in all modern history fully known to us."

In fact, we know more about Shakespeare's life than we do about almost any other English writer's of his era. His last will and testament (dated March 25, 1616) survives, as do numerous legal contracts and court documents involving Shakespeare as principal or witness, and parish records in Stratford and London. Shakespeare appears quite often in official records of King James's royal court, and of course Shakespeare's name appears on numerous title pages and in the written and recorded words of his literary contemporaries Robert Greene, Henry Chettle, Francis Meres, John Davies of Hereford, Ben Jonson, and many others. Indeed, if we make due allowance for the bloating of modern, run-of-the-mill bureaucratic records, more information has survived over the past four hundred years about William Shakespeare of Stratford-upon-Avon, Warwickshire, than is likely to survive in the next four hundred years about any reader of these words.

What we do not have are entire categories of information – Shakespeare's private letters or diaries, drafts and revisions of poems and plays, critical prefaces or essays, commendatory verse for other writers' works, or instructions guiding his fellow actors in their performances, for instance – that we imagine would help us understand and appreciate his surviving writings. For all we know, many such data never existed as written records. Many literary and theatrical critics, not knowing what might once have existed, more or less cheerfully accept the situation; some even make a theoretical virtue of it by claiming that such data are irrelevant to understanding and interpreting the plays and poems.

So, what do we know about William Shakespeare, the man responsible for thirty-seven or perhaps more plays, more than 150 sonnets, two lengthy narrative poems, and some shorter poems?

While many families by the name of Shakespeare (or some variant spelling) can be identified in the English Midlands as far back as the twelfth century, it seems likely that the dramatist's grandfather, Richard, moved to Snitterfield, a town not far from Stratford-upon-Avon, sometime before 1529. In Snitterfield, Richard Shakespeare leased farmland from the very wealthy Robert Arden. By 1552, Richard's son John had moved to a large house on Henley Street in Stratford-upon-Avon, the house that stands today as "The Birthplace." In Stratford, John Shakespeare traded as a glover, dealt in wool, and lent money at interest; he also served in a variety of civic posts, including "High Bailiff," the municipality's equivalent of mayor. In 1557, he married Robert Arden's youngest daughter, Mary. Mary and John had four sons – William was the oldest – and four daughters, of whom only Joan outlived her most celebrated sibling. William was baptized (an event entered in the Stratford parish church records) on April 26, 1564, and it has become customary, without any good factual support, to suppose he was born on April 23, which happens to be the feast day of Saint George, patron saint of England, and is also the date on which he died, in 1616. Shakespeare married Anne Hathaway in 1582, when he was eighteen and she was twenty-six; their first child was born five months later. It has been generally assumed that the marriage was enforced and subsequently unhappy, but these are only assumptions; it has been estimated, for instance, that up to one third of Elizabethan brides were pregnant when they married. Anne and William Shakespeare had three children: Susanna, who married a prominent local physician, John Hall; and the twins Hamnet, who died young in 1596, and Judith, who married Thomas Quiney – apparently a rather shady individual. The name Hamnet was unusual but not unique: he and his twin sister were named for their godparents, Shakespeare's neighbors Hamnet and Judith Sadler. Shakespeare's father died in 1601 (the year of *Hamlet*), and Mary Arden Shakespeare died in 1608 (the year of *Coriolanus*). William Shakespeare's last surviving direct descendant was his granddaughter Elizabeth Hall, who died in 1670.

Between the birth of the twins in 1585 and a clear reference to Shakespeare as a practicing London dramatist in Robert Greene's sensationalizing, satiric pamphlet, *Greene's Groatsworth of Wit* (1592), there is no record of where William Shakespeare was or what he was doing. These seven so-called lost years have been imaginatively filled by scholars and other students of Shakespeare: some think he traveled to Italy, or fought in the Low Countries, or studied law or medicine, or worked as an apprentice actor/writer, and so on to even more fanciful possibilities. Whatever the biographical facts for those "lost" years, Greene's nasty remarks in 1592 testify to professional envy and to the fact that Shakespeare already had a successful career in London. Speaking to his fellow playwrights, Greene warns both generally and specifically:

> . . . trust them [actors] not: for there is an upstart crow, beautified with our feathers, that with his tiger's heart wrapped in a player's hide supposes he is as well able to bombast out a blank verse as the best of you; and being an absolute Johannes Factotum, is in his own conceit the only Shake-scene in a country.

The passage mimics a line from *3 Henry VI* (hence the play must have been performed before Greene wrote) and seems to say that "Shake-scene" is both actor and playwright, a jack-of-all-trades. That same year, Henry Chettle protested Greene's remarks in *Kind-Heart's Dream,* and each of the next two years saw the publication of poems – *Venus and Adonis* and *The Rape of Lucrece,* respectively – publicly ascribed to (and dedicated by) Shakespeare. Early in 1595 he was named one of the senior members of a prominent acting company, the Lord Chamberlain's Men, when they received payment for court performances during the 1594 Christmas season.

Clearly, Shakespeare had achieved both success and reputation in London. In 1596, upon Shakespeare's application, the College of Arms granted his father the now-familiar coat of arms he had taken the first steps to obtain almost twenty years before, and in 1598, John's son – now permitted to call himself "gentleman" – took a 10 percent share in the new Globe playhouse. In 1597, he bought a substantial bourgeois house, called New Place, in Stratford – the garden remains, but Shakespeare's house, several times rebuilt, was torn down in 1759 – and over the next few years Shakespeare spent large sums buying land and making other investments in the town and its environs. Though he worked in London, his family remained in Stratford, and he seems always to have considered Stratford the home he would eventually return to. Something approaching a disinterested appreciation of Shakespeare's popular and professional status appears in Francis Meres's *Palladis Tamia* (1598), a not especially imaginative and perhaps therefore persuasive record of literary reputations. Reviewing contemporary English writers, Meres lists the titles of many of Shakespeare's plays, including one not now known, *Love's Labor's Won,* and praises his "mellifluous & hony-tongued" "sugred Sonnets," which were then circulating in manuscript (they were first collected in 1609). Meres describes Shakespeare as "one of the best" English playwrights of both comedy and tragedy. In *Remains . . . Concerning Britain* (1605), William Camden – a more authoritative source than the imitative Meres – calls Shakespeare one of the "most pregnant witts of these our times" and joins him with such writers as Chapman, Daniel, Jonson, Marston, and Spenser. During the first decades of the seventeenth century, publishers began to attribute numerous play quartos, including some non-Shakespearean ones, to Shakespeare, either by name or initials, and we may assume that they deemed Shakespeare's name and supposed authorship, true or false, commercially attractive.

For the next ten years or so, various records show

Shakespeare's dual career as playwright and man of the theater in London, and as an important local figure in Stratford. In 1608-9 his acting company – designated the "King's Men" soon after King James had succeeded Queen Elizabeth in 1603 – rented, refurbished, and opened a small interior playing space, the Blackfriars theater, in London, and Shakespeare was once again listed as a substantial sharer in the group of proprietors of the playhouse. By May 11, 1612, however, he describes himself as a Stratford resident in a London lawsuit – an indication that he had withdrawn from day-to-day professional activity and returned to the town where he had always had his main financial interests. When Shakespeare bought a substantial residential building in London, the Blackfriars Gatehouse, close to the theater of the same name, on March 10, 1613, he is recorded as William Shakespeare "of Stratford upon Avon in the county of Warwick, gentleman," and he named several London residents as the building's trustees. Still, he continued to participate in theatrical activity: when the new Earl of Rutland needed an allegorical design to bear as a shield, or *impresa,* at the celebration of King James's Accession Day, March 24, 1613, the earl's accountant recorded a payment of 44 shillings to Shakespeare for the device with its motto.

For the last few years of his life, Shakespeare evidently concentrated his activities in the town of his birth. Most of the final records concern business transactions in Stratford, ending with the notation of his death on April 23, 1616, and burial in Holy Trinity Church, Stratford-upon-Avon.

THE QUESTION OF AUTHORSHIP

The history of ascribing Shakespeare's plays (the poems do not come up so often) to someone else began, as it continues, peculiarly. The earliest published claim that someone else wrote Shakespeare's plays appeared in an 1856 article by Delia Bacon in the American journal *Putnam's Monthly* – although an Englishman, Thomas Wilmot, had shared his doubts in private (even secretive) conversations with friends near the end of the eighteenth century. Bacon's was a sad personal history that ended in madness and poverty, but the year after her article, she published, with great difficulty and the bemused assistance of Nathaniel Hawthorne (then United States Consul in Liverpool, England), her *Philosophy of the Plays of Shakspere Unfolded*. This huge, ornately written, confusing farrago is almost unreadable; sometimes its intents, to say nothing of its arguments, disappear entirely beneath near-raving, ecstatic writing. Tumbled in with much supposed "philosophy" appear the claims that Francis Bacon (from whom Delia Bacon eventually claimed descent), Walter Ralegh, and several other contemporaries of Shakespeare's had written the plays. The book had little impact except as a ridiculed curiosity.

Once proposed, however, the issue gained momentum among people whose conviction was the greater in proportion to their ignorance of sixteenth- and seventeenth-century English literature, history, and society. Another American amateur, Catherine P. Ashmead Windle, made the next influential contribution to the cause when she published *Report to the British Museum* (1882), wherein she promised to open "the Cipher of Francis Bacon," though what she mostly offers, in the words of S. Schoenbaum, is "demented allegorizing." An entire new cottage industry grew from Windle's suggestion that the texts contain hidden, cryptographically discoverable ciphers – "clues" – to their authorship; and today there are not only books devoted to the putative ciphers, but also pamphlets, journals, and newsletters.

Although Baconians have led the pack of those seeking a substitute Shakespeare, in *"Shakespeare" Identified* (1920), J. Thomas Looney became the first published

"Oxfordian" when he proposed Edward de Vere, seventeenth earl of Oxford, as the secret author of Shakespeare's plays. Also for Oxford and his "authorship" there are today dedicated societies, articles, journals, and books. Less popular candidates – Queen Elizabeth and Christopher Marlowe among them – have had adherents, but the movement seems to have divided into two main contending factions, Baconian and Oxfordian. (For further details on all the candidates for "Shakespeare," see S. Schoenbaum, *Shakespeare's Lives,* 2nd ed., 1991.)

The Baconians, the Oxfordians, and supporters of other candidates have one trait in common – they are snobs. Every pro-Bacon or pro-Oxford tract sooner or later claims that the historical William Shakespeare of Stratford-upon-Avon could not have written the plays because he could not have had the training, the university education, the experience, and indeed the imagination or background their author supposedly possessed. Only a learned genius like Bacon or an aristocrat like Oxford could have written such fine plays. (As it happens, lucky male children of the middle class had access to better education than most aristocrats in Elizabethan England – and Oxford was not particularly well educated.) Shakespeare received in the Stratford grammar school a formal education that would daunt many college graduates today; and popular rival playwrights such as the very learned Ben Jonson and George Chapman, both of whom also lacked university training, achieved great artistic success, without being taken as Bacon or Oxford.

Besides snobbery, one other quality characterizes the authorship controversy: lack of evidence. A great deal of testimony from Shakespeare's time shows that Shakespeare wrote Shakespeare's plays and that his contemporaries recognized them as distinctive and distinctly superior. (Some of that contemporary evidence is collected in E. K. Chambers, *William Shakespeare: A Study of Facts and Problems,* 2 vols., 1930.) Since that testimony comes from Shakespeare's enemies and theatrical competitors as well as from his co-workers and from the Elizabethan equivalent of literary journalists, it seems unlikely that, if any of these sources had known he was a fraud, they would have failed to record that fact.

Books About Shakespeare's Theater

Useful scholarly studies of theatrical life in Shakespeare's day include: G. E. Bentley, *The Jacobean and Caroline Stage,* 7 vols. (1941-68), and the same author's *The Professions of Dramatist and Player in Shakespeare's Time, 1590-1642* (1986); E. K. Chambers, *The Elizabethan Stage,* 4 vols. (1923); R. A. Foakes, *Illustrations of the English Stage, 1580-1642* (1985); Andrew Gurr, *The Shakespearean Stage,* 3rd ed. (1992), and the same author's *Play-going in Shakespeare's London,* 2nd ed. (1996); Edwin Nungezer, *A Dictionary of Actors* (1929); Carol Chillington Rutter, ed., *Documents of the Rose Playhouse* (1984).

Books About Shakespeare's Life

The following books provide scholarly, documented accounts of Shakespeare's life: G. E. Bentley, *Shakespeare: A Biographical Handbook* (1961); E. K. Chambers, *William Shakespeare: A Study of Facts and Problems,* 2 vols. (1930); S. Schoenbaum, *William Shakespeare: A Compact Documentary Life* (1977); and *Shakespeare's Lives,* 2nd ed. (1991), by the same author. Many scholarly editions of Shakespeare's complete works print brief compilations of essential dates and events. References to Shakespeare's works up to 1700 are collected in C. M. Ingleby et al., *The Shakespeare Allusion-Book,* rev. ed., 2 vols. (1932).

The Texts of Shakespeare

As FAR AS WE KNOW, only one manuscript conceivably in Shakespeare's own hand may (and even this is much disputed) exist: a few pages of a play called *Sir Thomas More,* which apparently was never performed. What we do have, as later readers, performers, scholars, students, are printed texts. The earliest of these survive in two forms: quartos and folios. Quartos (from the Latin for "four") are small books, printed on sheets of paper that were then folded in fours, to make eight double-sided pages. When these were bound together, the result was a squarish, eminently portable volume that sold for the relatively small sum of sixpence (translating in modern terms to about $5.00). In folios, on the other hand, the sheets are folded only once, in half, producing large, impressive volumes taller than they are wide. This was the format for important works of philosophy, science, theology, and literature (the major precedent for a folio Shakespeare was Ben Jonson's *Works,* 1616). The decision to print the works of a popular playwright in folio is an indication of how far up on the social scale the theatrical profession had come during Shakespeare's lifetime. The Shakespeare folio was an expensive book, selling for between fifteen and eighteen shillings, depending on the binding (in modern terms, from about $150 to $180). Twenty Shakespeare plays of the thirty-seven that survive first appeared in quarto, seventeen of which appeared during Shakespeare's lifetime; the rest of the plays are found only in folio.

The First Folio was published in 1623, seven years after Shakespeare's death, and was authorized by his fellow actors, the co-owners of the King's Men. This publication was certainly a mark of the company's enormous respect for Shakespeare; but it was also a way of turning the old plays, most of which were no longer current in the playhouse, into ready money (the folio includes only Shakespeare's plays, not his sonnets or other nondramatic verse). Whatever the motives behind the publication of the folio, the texts it preserves constitute the basis for almost all later editions of the playwright's works. The texts, however, differ from those of the earlier quartos, sometimes in minor respects but often significantly – most strikingly in the two texts of *King Lear,* but also in important ways in *Hamlet, Othello,* and *Troilus and Cressida.* (The variants are recorded in the textual notes to each play in the new Pelican series.) The differences in these texts represent, in a sense, the essence of theater: the texts of plays were initially not intended for publication. They were scripts, designed for the actors to perform – the principal life of the play at this period was in performance. And it follows that in Shakespeare's theater the playwright typically had no say either in how his play was performed or in the disposition of his text – he was an employee of the company. The authoritative figures in the theatrical enterprise were the shareholders in the company, who were for the most part the major actors. They decided what plays were to be done; they hired the playwright and often gave him an outline of the play they wanted him to write. Often, too, the play was a collaboration: the company would retain a group of writers, and parcel out the scenes among them. The resulting script was then the property of the company, and the actors would revise it as they saw fit during the course of putting it on stage. The resulting text belonged to the company. The playwright had no rights in it once he had been paid. (This system survives largely intact in the movie industry, and most of the playwrights of Shakespeare's time were as anonymous as most screenwriters are today.) The script could also, of course, continue to change as the tastes of audiences and the requirements of the actors changed. Many – perhaps most – plays were revised when they were reintroduced after any substantial absence from the repertory, or when they were performed by a company different from the one that originally commissioned the play.

Shakespeare was an exceptional figure in this world because he was not only a shareholder and actor in his company, but also its leading playwright – he was literally his own boss. He had, moreover, little interest in the publication of his plays, and even those that appeared during his lifetime with the authorization of the company show no signs of any editorial concern on the part of the author. Theater was, for Shakespeare, a fluid and supremely responsive medium – the very opposite of the great classic canonical text that has embodied his works since 1623.

The very fluidity of the original texts, however, has meant that Shakespeare has always had to be edited. Here is an example of how problematic the editorial project inevitably is, a passage from the most famous speech in *Romeo and Juliet,* Juliet's balcony soliloquy beginning "O Romeo, Romeo, wherefore art thou Romeo?" Since the eighteenth century, the standard modern text has read,

> What's Montague? It is nor hand, nor foot,
> Nor arm, nor face, nor any other part
> Belonging to a man. O be some other name!
> What's in a name? That which we call a rose
> By any other name would smell as sweet.
>
> (II.2.40–44)

Editors have three early texts of this play to work from, two quarto texts and the folio. Here is how the First Quarto (1597) reads:

> Whats *Mountague?* It is nor hand nor foote,
> Nor arme, nor face, nor any other part.
> Whats in a name? That which we call a Rose,
> By any other name would fmell as fweet:

Here is the Second Quarto (1599):

> Whats *Mountague?* it is nor hand nor foote,
> Nor arme nor face, ô be some other name
> Belonging to a man.
> Whats in a name that which we call a rose,
> By any other word would smell as sweete,

And here is the First Folio (1623):

> What's *Mountague?* it is nor hand nor foote,
> Nor arme, nor face, O be some other name
> Belonging to a man.
> What? in a names that which we call a Rose,
> By any other word would smell as sweete,

There is in fact no early text that reads as our modern text does – and this is the most famous speech in the play. Instead, we have three quite different texts, all of which are clearly some version of the same speech, but none of which seems to us a final or satisfactory version. The transcendently beautiful passage in modern editions is an editorial invention: editors have succeeded in conflating and revising the three versions into something we recognize as great poetry. Is this what Shakespeare "really" wrote? Who can say? What we can say is that Shakespeare always had performance, not a book, in mind.

Books About the Shakespeare Texts

The standard study of the printing history of the First Folio is W. W. Greg, *The Shakespeare First Folio* (1955). J. K. Walton, *The Quarto Copy for the First Folio of Shakespeare* (1971), is a useful survey of the relation of the quartos to the folio. The second edition of Charlton Hinman's *Norton Facsimile* of the First Folio (1996), with a new introduction by Peter Blayney, is indispensable. Stanley Wells, Gary Taylor, John Jowett, and William Montgomery, *William Shakespeare: A Textual Companion,* keyed to the Oxford text, gives a comprehensive survey of the editorial situation for all the plays and poems.

THE GENERAL EDITORS

Introduction

$A_{LL'S}$ WELL THAT ENDS WELL tests and unsettles our understanding of romantic comedy. While it technically belongs to the genre concerned with wooing and wedding, any play where the closing words of the heroine invoke the prospect of "Deadly divorce" (V.3.315) is bound to make us uneasy with (or nostalgic for) the harmony of hearts and social structures usually engineered by comedy. Comedy's concerns with renewal and regeneration, with the seductive fictions of love, and with the education of young people in the marital way of the world are all present in this play. So too it contains many of the elements of Shakespeare's other comedies: an enterprising heroine; a hero in need of tutelage; an older generation seeking to control the choices of its children; providential coincidences and conclusions. But unlike Shakespeare's earlier comedies, *All's Well That Ends Well* does not wear its conventions festively. A measure of the play's tenor can be taken from the words of its clown, Lavatch. When asked why he would marry, he replies, "My poor body, madam, requires it; I am driven on by the flesh; and he must needs go that the devil drives" (I.3.28-30). In this acknowledgment of bodily lust, and marriage as a clumsy social solution to an ethical problem, these lines rely for their humor upon the familiar injunction of Saint Paul (I Corinthians 7:9) that it is better to marry than to burn (either in lust or, consequently, in hell). But there is little of love's illusions or persuasions in this utilitarian recommendation, little sense of the seductive match of soul to soul that usually animates the dance of comedy.

It is perhaps a telling fact that a comedy's clown appears "A shrewd knave and an unhappy" (IV.5.62). Shakespeare's clowns can often be melancholy or even curmudgeonly, but the strain of sadness that permeates Lavatch's humor is particularly mournful – indeed, he is in mourning, for his dead master and his aging mistress. It is an existential sadness that finds its way into the play's atmosphere at large, so concerned as the play is with the less than joyful aspects of human identity. The darkness of the tone as much as anything else has provided us with a guess as to this play's date of composition. Unprinted and unregistered until 1623, with the publication of the First Folio, *All's Well That Ends Well* has been grouped with two other of Shakespeare's darker, or "problem," comedies, *Troilus and Cressida* and *Measure for Measure,* thought to have been written in the years 1602-4, when Shakespeare was also beginning to explore the worlds of his high tragedies. These plays are loosely concerned with the experience of romantic love, and hence technically comic; however, the conventional workings of comedy are troubled by the manifold failures of human character. Their conclusions are more compromised than in traditional comedy, but less cathartic than in traditional tragedy: hence, problematic. Stylistic considerations also argue for dating *All's Well* to this moment in Shakespeare's career.

As in these other two plays, love is a thorny proposition in *All's Well That Ends Well;* while the vision of union is perhaps not as diseased as it appears in *Measure* or as degraded as it appears in *Troilus,* the power of this play to confront the psychic as well as the social obstacles to love's success makes it an unusually self-conscious experience of comic promise. Human flaws are prominently in evidence: willfulness, snobbery, coercion, and bombast, just to name the most conspicuous. As the younger brother Dumaine (called the "Second Lord") comments to the elder (the "First Lord"), "As we are ourselves, what things are we!" (IV.3.19-20) – meaning that without divine assistance, human beings are a sorry lot indeed.

At the same time, perhaps more so than the other two plays, *All's Well That Ends Well* does provide a vision of forgiveness and even potential reformation that, however painful, approaches the transformative power of Shakespeare's late plays. This play frustrates romantic plots, but it also fulfills them, after a fashion. For despite the presence in the play of characters who swear – and fall – by an unadorned human power, it is also true that Shakespeare repeatedly calls our attention to a beneficent divine protection against our own worst wills. *All's Well That Ends Well* meditates on the interplay of divine grace and human will that engineers the compromises that pass for human happiness. The necessity for both these agencies results from the double character of human nature itself: as the younger Dumaine also observes, "The web of our life is of a mingled yarn, good and ill together; our virtues would be proud if our faults whipped them not, and our crimes would despair if they were not cherished by our virtues" (IV.3.70-73). Throughout the play we are confronted with the compound quality of human nature.

Helena is a prime example of the mingled nature of human identity and the intersection, and intercession, of powers necessary to save it from itself. Like many of Shakespeare's female protagonists, she must pursue her beloved with a singular purpose and against more than usual odds: her beloved Count Rossillion is not merely uncouth but ungracious, finding her ludicrous as a prospective mate, due to her lowly birth as a poor physician's daughter. He disdains her despite her obvious virtue and beauty, and the persuasion of his king and mother. Helena's ambition in seeking to "lose [her virginity] to her own liking" (I.1.151-52) is both admirable in its enterprise and repellent in its presumption (not once does she consider what Bertram might feel about her as a wife). In her plan to barter a cure for the ailing king in exchange for Bertram's hand she must engage both her own resources and those of heaven. Helena initially believes in her own ability to achieve her goals: "Our remedies oft in ourselves do lie, / Which we ascribe to heaven" (214-15). At the same time, she acknowledges the role of divine power in effecting her desires: "most it is presumption in us," she tells the king, "when / The help of heaven we count the act of men" (II.1.152-53). It must be said, however, that the latter acknowledgment of divine assistance is far more prominent after her initial plan to secure Bertram's love has failed. Or rather, after she realizes that while her own ingenuity may be sufficient to marry her to Bertram, it will not serve as a means to his loving her.

For like someone who has been reading too many fairy tales about poor but deserving heroines who make good, Helena believes that virtue can triumph, Cinderella-like, over social obstacles. She asks herself, "Who ever strove / To show her merit that did miss her love?" (I.1.224-25). Indeed, in this play, virtue does in part triumph: her desire is sanctioned both by the family of her beloved and the king. But the obstacles to love's fulfillment here are not social, but psychic. Neither parents nor politics stand in the way of this marriage. But while the social barriers to the union of Helena and Bertram can be removed by the powers – ruler and family – that sustain them, what these powers cannot do is change the way in which Bertram's character has been shaped by them. Bertram actively disdains her, not for who she is, but for what she is: beneath him. And as with many Renaissance male literary lovers who, seduced by their own vision of love, are blinded to the reality of the beloved, Helena fails to acknowledge that just because she loves someone doesn't necessarily mean that he loves her in return. Love is not a meritocracy – not least because no matter how virtuous a human being may be, the very condition of being human bespeaks the failures of original sin. God does not love us (or so this play suggests) because we deserve to be loved; he loves us despite the fact that we do not so deserve.

The humiliation and education of the recalcitrant and proud Bertram is a chief concern of the play; he is caught in a lie, in an offense to his family honor, and in disgrace. He is saved from his own venality only by virtue of Helena's capacity to forgive and outmaneuver him, a capacity that both mimics the agile operations of divine providence and owes its success to them. While there can be a certain amount of sympathy for Bertram's initial predicament, being forced as he is to marry against his will, his subsequent conduct magnifies the unpleasantness of his initial snobbery and churlishness. His parting, riddling challenge to his wife – that he will never acknowledge her as such until she procures the family ring he wears and produces a child of his own fathering – maliciously taunts her to wrest things from him that he ought to bestow gladly upon her, and which, presumably, she cannot procure without his cooperation (aptly, what she had neglected to solicit in the first place). Perhaps most painful of all, he even makes her beg for a farewell kiss. Thus given his cruelty to Helena, whom he refuses to bed, and to Diana, whom he believes he has seduced with a promise to wed (only to then publicly call her a "common gamester," V.3.187, when she asks him to fulfill it), there is a certain satisfaction to his comeuppance. (It could however be said in Bertram's defense that were the genders reversed in this play – were a young woman coerced by her king to marry against her will – modern sympathies would be far more likely to ally themselves with her than they do with Bertram.) At the end of the play, confused, outwitted, and teetering on the brink of social disgrace, Bertram is forced into an acknowledgment of his dependence on powers and graces beyond his control. He is not, in fact, as bad a person as he himself believed himself to be: due to Helena's intervention, he has not seduced and abandoned an innocent maiden (rather he has abandoned, and then seduced, his own wife).

But Helena's own convictions of her lovability are also shaken, and need to be, in a play that so fiercely interrogates the claims of self-worth in a creature so inherently flawed as a human being. After enduring Bertram's intentionally cruel rejection of her, Helena wins his acquiescence to their marriage – though not, necessarily, his love – only by fulfilling a series of humiliating tests that would tax the emotional and practical resources of the most able chivalric questant. Having once prided herself on her own resourcefulness even as she nodded to a reliance on divine grace, Helena is forced to exercise both to their utmost limit. Her pilgrimage and her rebirth are emotional as well as literal events. Not only must she find her runaway husband, maneuver herself incognito into his bed, acquire his treasured family ring, and – perhaps hardest of all – experience his lovemaking in the guise of another woman, but she must also trust that this one sexual encounter will be sufficient for the conception of the child without which Bertram has sworn he will never acknowledge her. She achieves all these goals through a paradoxical combination of self-abnegation and guile, but it is the last miracle whose success must acknowledge above all the power of providence as well as of pluck. At the end of the play, much like Milton's Adam and Eve after the Fall, the two spouses meet each other on the equal ground of a hard-earned humility achieved through a mutually inflicted suffering.

Worth – where does it lie, how is it imagined and known? Does it come from one's family? One's morals? One's friends? What is the relation between virtue and power, ethical worth and social rank, goodness and "blood"? In a world bedeviled by original sin, can any human being claim to be worthy? *All's Well That Ends Well* repeatedly ponders this question, and troubles the answers. Bertram is told when he arrives at the king's court that his dead father was esteemed for his conspicuous disregard for social rank in the evaluation of less socially fortunate persons, a gentleman in the ethical as well as the political dimension: "Who were below him / He used as creatures of another place, / And bowed his eminent top to their low ranks, / Making them proud of his humility" (I.2.41–44). Yet if his father, a nobleman, was admirable for pretending that social distinctions did not exist, Bertram cannot ignore them, as his own will is subject to that of his king (to ignore rank is easier the more powerful one is). The king tells Bertram that he alone creates honor, and can confer it, if he so chooses, on whomever he wishes (i.e., Helena): "'Tis only title thou disdain'st in her, the which / I can build up" (II.3.116-17). The king claims, ideally enough, that "Honors thrive / When rather from our acts we them derive / Than our foregoers" (134-36). In other words, deeds, not dads, create our worth. But this is easy for him to say; Bertram's snobbery is, in another light, a form of social obedience.

There is thus something disingenuous about the position that holds that virtue is independent of social identity. Helena, for instance, can cure the king only because she possesses one of her physician father's special remedies, and it is that, not her youth, beauty, or the fact that she is a good person, that makes her valuable to the king (in fact, had she not wanted to win Bertram's hand in marriage, the thought of curing the king of his illness might not have even arisen in her). So too Bertram's snobbish behavior is a direct result of his high birth. It is also true that the king's ennobling of Helena violates the principle of the very distinction between gentle and base blood that royalty upholds and by which Bertram has been reared. The king's instantaneous creation of Helena's nobility merely reveals how arbitrary notions of worth based on social power are. On the other hand, Helena's nobility of character is unrecognizable to Bertram – or at least unconvincing as a rationale for his marriage to her. (Helena is not the only one who wishes to marry to her own liking.) The king may claim that "Good alone / Is good without a name" (II.3.127-28), but this seems an impossibly naive sentiment in a world structured by political rank; as far as Bertram's marriage is concerned, it is a singularly irrelevant one.

It must be said that Bertram is a particularly unastute judge of human value, however it is construed. His recognition of Helena as his worthy wife, if indeed it is ever to occur, requires a prior education in the protocols of knowing and judging. If his moral education takes place anywhere in the play, it is in his coming to know not the

worthiness of Helena, but the unworthiness of his companion Parolles – and by association, the unworthiness of
his own judgment in having esteemed him.

Bertram's inability to know others (and presumably
himself) is underscored by the fact that the worth, or lack
thereof, of Parolles is glaringly obvious to every other
character in the play. This discrepant awareness creates a
kind of dramatic irony internal to the play, by which not
merely the audience but all the characters are in possession of a knowledge at which we wait for Bertram to also
arrive. In the first scene, Helena tells us upon Parolles' entrance, "I know him a notorious liar, / Think him a great
way fool, solely a coward" (I.1.102-3). Her opinion is
shared by the other members of Bertram's household, the
clown and the Countess Rossillion. At court, the Lord
Lafew immediately spots him for an impostor, and in war,
so do Bertram's fellow soldiers: "Believe it, my lord, in
mine own direct knowledge, without any malice, but to
speak of him as my kinsman, he's a most notable coward,
an infinite and endless liar, an hourly promise-breaker, the
owner of no one good quality worthy your lordship's entertainment" (III.6.7-12). The name Parolles translates,
from the French, as "words" (*paroles*) – as opposed to
deeds – and in Parolles Shakespeare animates the convention of the braggart soldier, or *miles gloriosus:* scarves,
flags, drums, and bombast, but beneath all the noise, a
cowardly heart. Bertram is perhaps only able to know
Parolles as such once Bertram has distinguished himself in
war, a process that argues for the necessity of experience in
forming judgment. Bertram cannot judge without his
own direct knowledge of what it takes to be brave in
deeds as well as in words.

But what is strange about the exposure of Parolles is
that it is not exclusively his cowardice or disloyalty that
causes Bertram finally to disdain him. For in addition to
being revealed as a coward, Parolles reveals Bertram as "a
foolish idle boy, but for all that very ruttish" (IV.3.211).
Bombastic though Parolles' words may be, some of them

hit home. Tellingly, Bertram's singularly feeble disavowal of Parolles refers not to his cowardice but to what Bertram perceives as Parolles' spitefulness in speaking against him: "now he's a cat to me"(234). Parolles tells a kind of truth about Bertram, for the latter's recently acquired military honor has no bearing on his possession of honor in other domains. Furthermore, Parolles shares with the most engaging of Shakespeare's cowards, Falstaff, the ability to speak the truth about himself. He knows himself a braggart, foolish with words and boasts, and even has the grace to regret it: "Who knows himself a braggart, / Let him fear this; for it will come to pass / That every braggart shall be found an ass" (324-26). Parolles, at least, comes to be under no illusions about his own bravery, honor, or lovability. While he may be unsavory, he is in the end neither unknowing nor unashamed.

The value and use of self-knowledge are thus a central concern of this play. What does it profit one, if anything, to know oneself? – especially given the fact that all persons are, in a Christian universe, inevitably flawed, and perhaps irremediably so if left only to their own devices. To know oneself, according to a Christian understanding of the self, is above all to know oneself imperfect. But does knowledge of one's own faults work to remedy them in any way? Does self-knowledge lead to remedy or merely to ruefulness? The younger Dumaine, or "Second Lord," who supplies much of the play's moral reflections (oddly enough, despite his relatively minor status name and few lines), is amazed that Parolles can both know himself and continue to be himself, that shame does not produce a change of character: "Is it possible he should know what he is, and be that he is?"(IV.1.43-44). These lines recognize a certain abstract quality to the self-knowledge of one's own unworthiness. For it is doubtful whether Parolles' exposure to himself, or to Bertram, as a coward has any corrective function for either character. And while Bertram is discomfited to hear about his own "ruttishness," it is not clear that hearing about it profits him in any way or prevents him from continuing to be ruttish. Self-knowledge seems thus an engaging but not necessarily dynamic fact of human identity. Hence perhaps Parolles' undaunted cheer when exposed: "Simply the thing I am / Shall make me live. . . . Parolles, live / Safest in shame; being fooled, by foolery thrive. / There's place and means for every man alive" (IV.3.323-29).

The hope, of course, of a Christian ethics and one perhaps of this play is that knowledge of a fault is the first requisite of its amendment, or at least the necessary precondition of knowing oneself dependent upon a higher moral agency (or, if you are Parolles, upon the service of Lord Lafew). It is telling that the revelation of Parolles' qualities does not, in fact, serve to exile him from the community of the comedy (unlike, say, *Twelfth Night*'s Malvolio). Why should he be? He may be flawed, but so aren't we all, and at least he knows himself to be such and has the grace to be ashamed of it (at least temporarily). Shame, it seems, is the goal of this comedy's process: producing it, commemorating it, and making its chastening effect a lasting and perhaps an ameliorating one. The shaming of Bertram is especially severe, perhaps because his role in the comedy – husband – requires the hope of his reformation, and perhaps also because other characters would prefer to think his ignoble behavior a function of Parolles' companionship, rather than inherent to Bertram himself. Nobility in deed as well as in name requires a scapegoat nonetheless.

A play invested in producing shame is not necessarily a pleasant experience for the audience or its characters. In this regard, *All's Well That Ends Well* belongs to the class of satiric comedies designed to eradicate pretension and leave in its place a scourged humility and, perhaps, a hope of reformation, so as to prepare the way to what the clown Lavatch, after Matthew 7:13-14, calls "the house with the narrow gate, which I take to be too little for pomp to enter" (IV.5.50-51). The reformation required for entrance to the heavenly kingdom of the righteous (as opposed to "the flowery way that leads to the broad gate and the great fire," 53-54) is partly a function of human effort. Yet human resources alone are not enough to complete the journey. Even as the human nature this play contemplates is of a mingled kind, and relies on both self and providence to secure its salvation, so too the play partakes formally of the marvelous as well as the sardonic modes, the folktale as well as the satire.

Shakespeare works out his thematic concerns in the architecture of his play. Much as the double generic register of the play articulates its ethical assumptions, the contrasting worlds of the play further express the mixed nature of human experience. The action takes place in a series of paired but opposed locations: Rossillion and the court; France and Italy; and, within Italy, the male world of war and the female community of Florence. The first half of the play, set in France, is the more satiric: it is the exhausted world of the old, of death and dying. Two recently dead fathers, a mortally ill king, and a bereaved and aging countess dominate the comic landscape. It is clearly a universe in need of generational renewal (hence perhaps the ready collusion of both king and mother in Helena's ambitions for Bertram; hence too the Lord Lafew's nearly pornographic vision of youth's power in the person of Helena: "whose simple touch / Is powerful to araise King Pepin, nay, / To give great Charlemagne a pen in's hand, / And write to her a love line," II.1.76-79). With the exception of Helena, whose vision of love belongs to the idealizing registers of Petrarchan poetry, the motors of generational renewal – marriage and sexuality – appear in a grimly misogynistic light of male violence and female perfidy. Parolles tells Helena that virginity is a stale quantity – it "breeds mites, much like a cheese"; it is like French withered pears: "it looks ill, it eats drily" (I.1.143, 162) – but his jokes are equally outworn, and a similar tenor afflicts the play's larger sense of regenerative buoyancy. Helena seems quite alone in her romantic enthusiasm, which the older generation views with an almost vampiric desire. But although her language is also formulaic, belonging to the register of Petrarchan idealism, the play strains to endorse it, even as it seeks to banish Parolles' cynicism. For if this is to be a comedy, even a fragile one, Helena's vision must ultimately, however provisionally, triumph.

Thus with Act III, scene 5 we move to Italy, to the "brave wars" (II.1.25) and a scene of romance unfettered by an older generation. Indeed, though a war is potentially a grim and death-driven backdrop, its chief function in the play is as site of youthful exploit, both military and romantic (though there is something unnerving about a vision of war as a mere "Nursery to our gentry, who are sick / For breathing and exploit," I.2.16–17). The King of France sends his followers off to war not with thoughts for their souls or their honors, so much as their hearts: "Those girls of Italy, take heed of them. / They say our French lack language to deny / If they demand; beware of being captives / Before you serve" (II.1.19–22). The Italian world is one of comparative youth, bravery, parades, and conquests. It is, despite the war, a conspicuously feminine world. Bertram's wooing of Diana is in its way quite hackneyed (that, too, bears the imprint of Parolles), but there is perhaps something just slightly less grotesque about his leers than his mentor's ('tis new to him). This world is not without its disillusionments: Diana loses her innocence as much as Helena or Bertram do ("Since Frenchmen are so braid, / Marry that will, I live and die a maid," IV.2.73–74). But there is a sense of larger, more generous, and generative, forces at work – forces that come primarily through the beneficent agency of female community. Although the women are not schemers in the way that the King of France imagines them to be, they do indeed take Bertram captive, and confront him with a riddle of their own, one that asks him to contemplate the value of his own worth: "Because he's guilty, and he is not guilty" (V.3.286). Confronted with his resurrected wife, who bears both his child and his family ring, Bertram must acknowledge that forces larger than himself are at work.

The argument of this play (if a play can argue anything) is that, like Bertram, humans are both guilty and not guilty: guilty of our own doing, and saved from that guilt, or at least its worst effects, by both providence and our own best selves. Bertram's final words to Helena may be only a conditional promise to love her as he should: "If she, my liege, can make me know this clearly, / I'll love her dearly – ever, ever dearly" (312-13). They derive from a sense of shame as well as relief: shame at his own behavior, and relief that he has been saved, due to Helena and heaven's agency, from its own worst effects. His reformation is by no means complete – indeed, it has barely begun. But in the play's acknowledgment of the possibilities of both love and knowledge, *All's Well That Ends Well* makes a case for the best as well as the worst in all of us.

CLAIRE MCEACHERN
University of California, Los Angeles

Note on the Text

ALL'S WELL THAT ENDS WELL was first published in the folio of 1623, with Shakespeare's own draft evidently serving as printer's copy. Although marred by certain misprints and minor irregularities, it is a reasonably good text and has been followed closely in the present edition. The folio text is divided into acts corresponding with those in modern editions, but not into scenes. The act-scene division here supplied for reference purposes is the conventional one evolved by Shakespeare's editors. All material departures from the folio text are listed below, with the adopted reading in italics followed by the folio reading in roman.

I.1 **39** *promises. Her* (Rowe³) promises her   **76 s.d.** *[To Helena]* (Rowe¹) (not in F)   **89** *above me.* (Rowe: me:) me   **95** *hour, to* (Pope) houre to   **130** *got* goe   **148** *within the* (Harrison) within ten   **159** *wear* (Capell) were

I.2 **3 s.p.** FIRST LORD (Rowe¹) Lo.G (throughout)   **15 s.p.** SECOND LORD (Rowe¹) Lo.E (throughout)   **18** *Rossillion* Rosingoll

I.3 **19** *and I will* and w will   **59–62** (as verse) (Rowe³) (as prose in F)   **84** *An* (Pope) and   **85** *but or* (Capell) but ore   **111** *level; [Diana no]* (Theobald¹) levell, Queen   **133–34** *Helen, / I* (Capell) (as one line in F)   **135–36** *Nay . . . mother. / Why . . . mother?* (Pope) (as one line in F)   **167** *loneliness* (Theobald¹) louelinesse   **173** *t' one to th' other* (F2: 'ton) 'ton tooth to th' other   **189–90** *heaven, / I* (Pope) (as one line in F)   **198** *intenible* (F2) intemible   **245** *and* (F3:, and) , an

II.1 **3** *gain all* (Johnson) gain, all   **44** *with his cicatrix, an emblem* (Theobald¹) his sicatrice, with an Emblem   **48** *you* (Hanmer) ye   **63** *fee* (Theobald¹) see   **110** *dear; I have* (Var. '78: dear, I); dear I   **156** *impostor* (F3) imposture   **174** *nay* (Singer²) ne   **193** *heaven* (Theobald¹ conj. Thirlby) helpe

II.2 **55–56** (as verse) (Knight¹) (as prose in F)   **58** *An* (Rowe³) And

II.3 **75 s.d.** *She addresses . . . Lord* (appears after l. 61 in F)   **93** *her* here   **124** *when* (Theobald¹ conj. Thirlby) whence   **129** *it is* is is   **140** *indeed. What* (Theobald¹) indeed, what   **290** *detested* (Rowe¹) detected

II.4 **35** *me? [. . .] The* (Hunter) me? Clo. The

II.5 **26** *End* (Collier¹) And

III.1 **23** *to the* to'th the

III.2 9 *sold* (F3) hold   18 *E'en* (Theobald[1]) In   64 *engrossest all* (F4) en-grossest, all   108 *still-piecing* (Var. '78 conj. Anon.) still peering

III.4 7 *have* hane

III.5 33 *le* (F3) la

III.6 35 *his* (Rowe[1]) this   36 *ore* (Theobald[1]) ours

III.7 19 *Resolved* (Collier[1]) Resolue

IV.1 88 *art* (F3) are

IV.2 38 *may . . . snare* (Sisson conj. Daniel) make . . . scarre

IV.3 81–83 *They . . . midnight* (assigned to Cap. G in F3) (assigned to Bertram in F)   89 *effected* (F3) affected

IV.3 117 FIRST LORD *Hush, hush!* (Dyce[2] conj. W. S. Walker) (assigned to Bertram in F)   137 BERTRAM *All's . . . him* (Capell) (assigned to Parolles in F)   192 *lordship* (Pope) Lord   235 *the* (F3) your   258 *him!* (Alexander) him

IV.4 3 *'fore* (F2) for   9 *Marseilles* (Rowe[3]) Marcellae   16 *you* (F4) your

IV.5 21 *grass* (Rowe[1]) grace   39 *name* (Rowe[1]) maine   78 *Marseilles* (Pope) Marcellus

V.1 6 s.d. *Gentleman* (F3) gentle Astringer

V.2 24 *similes* (Theobald[1] conj. Warburton) smiles   32 *under her* (F2) under

V.3 58–59 *carried, . . . sender* (Theobald[1]) carried . . . sender,   71 s.p. COUNTESS (Theobald) (assigned to King in F)   122 *tax* taze   154 *sir, sith* (Tyrwhitt: sir, since) sir, sir   182 *them. Fairer* (Theobald: them; Fairer) them fairer   206 *sickens but . . . truth* (Hanmer) sickens: but . . . truth,   215 *infinite cunning* (Singer[2] conj. W. S. Walker) insuite coming   257 *that,* (F3) that   310 *are* is

All's Well That Ends Well

[NAMES OF THE ACTORS

KING OF FRANCE
DUKE OF FLORENCE
BERTRAM, *Count of Rossillion*
LAFEW, *an old lord*
PAROLLES, *a follower of Bertram*
RINALDO, *steward to the Countess of Rossillion*
LAVATCH, *a clown in her household*
A PAGE *in her household*
COUNTESS OF ROSSILLION, *mother to Bertram*
HELENA, *orphaned daughter of the countess's physician*
WIDOW CAPILET, *of Florence*
DIANA, *her daughter*
VIOLENTA ⎱ *neighbors and friends to the widow*
MARIANA ⎰
LORDS, ATTENDANTS, SOLDIERS, MESSENGERS, *etc.,*
    French and Florentine

SCENE: *Rossillion, Paris,*
    Florence, Marseilles]
    *

All's Well That
Ends Well

∾ **I.1.** *Enter young Bertram, Count of Rossillion, his*
Mother [the Countess], and Helena; Lord Lafew – all
in black.

COUNTESS   In delivering my son from me I bury a sec- 1
ond husband.

BERTRAM   And I in going, madam, weep o'er my father's
death anew; but I must attend his majesty's command,
to whom I am now in ward, evermore in subjection. 5

LAFEW   You shall find of the king a husband, madam;
you, sir, a father. He that so generally is at all times 7
good must of necessity hold his virtue to you, whose 8
worthiness would stir it up where it wanted, rather 9
than lack it where there is such abundance. 10

COUNTESS   What hope is there of his majesty's amend- 11
ment?

LAFEW   He hath abandoned his physicians, madam,
under whose practices he hath persecuted time with 14
hope, and finds no other advantage in the process but
only the losing of hope by time.

COUNTESS   This young gentlewoman had a father – O,
that "had," how sad a passage 'tis – whose skill was al- 18

I.1 The palace of the Countess of Rossillion   1 *delivering* sending off (with
pun on "giving birth to")   5 *to . . . ward* whose ward I now am   7 *generally*
i.e., to all men   8 *hold* maintain   9 *wanted* was absent   10 *lack* fail to
arouse   11–12 *amendment* recovery   14 *persecuted time* painfully prolonged
in living   18 *passage* phrase (with pun on "passing away")

19   most as great as his honesty; had it stretched so far,
20   would have made nature immortal, and death should
     have play for lack of work. Would for the king's sake he
     were living! I think it would be the death of the king's
     disease.

LAFEW   How called you the man you speak of, madam?

COUNTESS   He was famous, sir, in his profession, and it
     was his great right to be so – Gerard de Narbon.

LAFEW   He was excellent indeed, madam. The king very
     lately spoke of him admiringly and mourningly. He
29   was skillful enough to have lived still, if knowledge
30   could be set up against mortality.

BERTRAM   What is it, my good lord, the king languishes
     of?

33 LAFEW   A fistula, my lord.

BERTRAM   I heard not of it before.

LAFEW   I would it were not notorious. Was this gentle-
     woman the daughter of Gerard de Narbon?

COUNTESS   His sole child, my lord, and bequeathed to
38   my overlooking. I have those hopes of her good that
     her education promises. Her dispositions she inherits,
40   which makes fair gifts fairer; for where an unclean
41   mind carries virtuous qualities, there commendations
42   go with pity – they are virtues and traitors too. In her
43   they are the better for their simpleness. She derives
     her honesty and achieves her goodness.

LAFEW   Your commendations, madam, get from her
     tears.

47 COUNTESS   'Tis the best brine a maiden can season her
     praise in. The remembrance of her father never ap-
     proaches her heart but the tyranny of her sorrows takes
50   all livelihood from her cheek. No more of this, Helena.

---

19 *so far* i.e., as his honesty   **29** *still* forever   **33** *fistula* an ulcerous sore   **38** *overlooking* supervision (i.e., Helena is a ward, as Bertram is)   **41** *qualities* aspects   **42** *go* i.e., simultaneously   **43** *simpleness* being unmixed with vice; *derives* inherits   **47** *season* preserve   **50** *livelihood* sign of life (i.e., color)

Go to, no more, lest it be rather thought you affect a   51
sorrow than to have –

HELENA   *[Aside]* I do affect a sorrow indeed, but I have it
too.

LAFEW   Moderate lamentation is the right of the dead,
excessive grief the enemy to the living.

COUNTESS   If the living be enemy to the grief, the excess   57
makes it soon mortal.

BERTRAM   Madam, I desire your holy wishes.   59

LAFEW   How understand we that?   60

COUNTESS
Be thou blessed, Bertram, and succeed thy father
In manners, as in shape. Thy blood and virtue   62
Contend for empire in thee, and thy goodness
Share with thy birthright. Love all, trust a few,
Do wrong to none. Be able for thine enemy   65
Rather in power than use, and keep thy friend   66
Under thy own life's key. Be checked for silence,   67
But never taxed for speech. What heaven more will,   68
That thee may furnish, and my prayers pluck down,
Fall on thy head! – Farewell, my lord.   70
'Tis an unseasoned courtier. Good my lord,   71
Advise him.   72

LAFEW   He cannot want the best
That shall attend his love.

COUNTESS   Heaven bless him! Farewell, Bertram.
                                                   [Exit.]

BERTRAM   The best wishes that can be forged in your
thoughts be servants to you! *[To Helena]* Be comfort-   76
able to my mother, your mistress, and make much of
her.

---

51 *affect* pretend   **57–58** *If . . . mortal* unless the living actively combat the
grief, the excess of grief will soon prove fatal to them   **59** *wishes* blessings
62 *blood* (1) lineage, (2) unruly passion   **65** *able* a match   **66** *in power* potentially; *use* as a matter of habit   **66–67** *keep . . . key* defend your friend's life
as you would your own   **67** *checked* reproved   **68** *taxed for speech* rebuked for
chattering   **71** *unseasoned* inexperienced   **72–73** *want . . . love* lack the best
advice that shall accompany my love for him   **76–77** *comfortable* comforting

79 LAFEW Farewell, pretty lady. You must hold the credit of
80   your father.   *[Exeunt Bertram and Lafew.]*
    HELENA
        O, were that all! I think not on my father,
        And these great tears grace his remembrance more
83   Than those I shed for him. What was he like?
        I have forgot him. My imagination
85   Carries no favor in't but Bertram's.
        I am undone; there is no living, none,
        If Bertram be away. 'Twere all one
        That I should love a bright particular star
89   And think to wed it, he is so above me.
90   In his bright radiance and collateral light
91   Must I be comforted, not in his sphere.
92   Th' ambition in my love thus plagues itself:
93   The hind that would be mated by the lion
94   Must die for love. 'Twas pretty, though a plague,
        To see him every hour, to sit and draw
96   His archèd brows, his hawking eye, his curls,
97   In our heart's table – heart too capable
98   Of every line and trick of his sweet favor.
        But now he's gone, and my idolatrous fancy
100   Must sanctify his relics. Who comes here?
            Enter Parolles.
101   One that goes with him; I love him for his sake,
        And yet I know him a notorious liar,
103   Think him a great way fool, solely a coward.
104   Yet these fixed evils sit so fit in him

---

79 *hold* uphold 83 *those . . . him* i.e., when he died 85 *favor* face 89
above i.e., in social rank 90 *collateral* i.e., shed from above (the stars of
Bertram and Helena move in parallel orbits, his higher one shedding *collateral light* on her lower one) 91 *his sphere* his own orbit 92 *plagues itself* becomes its own tormentor 93 *hind* female deer 94 *pretty . . . plague*
pleasant, though painful 96 *hawking* hawklike 97 *table* drawing tablet
97–98 *capable / Of* readily impressed with 98 *trick* trait; *favor* features
100 *sanctify* make holy, worship, enshrine; *relics* remains (as those of a saint)
101 *his* Bertram's 103 *a great way* very much a; *solely* all 104 *sit so fit* are so
well lodged

That they take place when virtue's steely bones   105
Looks bleak i' th' cold wind; withal, full oft we see   106
Cold wisdom waiting on superfluous folly.   107

PAROLLES   Save you, fair queen!

HELENA   And you, monarch!

PAROLLES   No.   110

HELENA   And no.

PAROLLES   Are you meditating on virginity?

HELENA   Ay. You have some stain of soldier in you; let   113
me ask you a question. Man is enemy to virginity; how
may we barricado it against him?

PAROLLES   Keep him out.

HELENA   But he assails, and our virginity, though valiant,
in the defense yet is weak. Unfold to us some warlike
resistance.

PAROLLES   There is none. Man setting down before you   120
will undermine you and blow you up.   121

HELENA   Bless our poor virginity from underminers and
blowers-up! Is there no military policy how virgins
might blow up men?

PAROLLES   Virginity being blown down, man will quick-
lier be blown up; marry, in blowing him down again,   126
with the breach yourselves made you lose your city. It is
not politic in the commonwealth of nature to preserve   128
virginity. Loss of virginity is rational increase, and there   129
was never virgin got till virginity was first lost. That you   130
were made of is metal to make virgins. Virginity by   131
being once lost may be ten times found; by being ever   132
kept it is ever lost. 'Tis too cold a companion. Away
with't!

105–6 *when . . . wind* when virtue looks puritanical and forbidding **106**
withal consequently   **107** *waiting on* dancing attendance upon; *superfluous*
i.e., overdressed **113** *stain* tinge **120** *setting down before* besieging **121**
blow you up (with pun on "impregnate") **126** *blown up* i.e., reinflated, given
an erection; *marry* indeed (originally an oath on the name of the Virgin Mary)
126–27 *in . . . city* in quenching his lust (by yielding) you lose the fortress of
your virginity **128** *politic* statesmanlike **129** *rational increase* reasonable rate
of population growth **130** *got* begotten; *That* that which **131** *metal* sub-
stance **132** *may . . . found* i.e., may engender ten more virgins

135 HELENA   I will stand for't a little, though therefore I die a
        virgin.

137 PAROLLES   There's little can be said in't; 'tis against the
138   rule of nature. To speak on the part of virginity is to ac-
139   cuse your mothers, which is most infallible disobedi-
140   ence. He that hangs himself is a virgin; virginity
141   murders itself, and should be buried in highways out of
        all sanctified limit, as a desperate offendress against na-
143   ture. Virginity breeds mites, much like a cheese, con-
144   sumes itself to the very paring, and so dies with feeding
        his own stomach. Besides, virginity is peevish, proud,
146   idle, made of self-love, which is the most inhibited sin
147   in the canon. Keep it not; you cannot choose but lose
148   by't. Out with't! within the year it will make itself two,
149   which is a goodly increase, and the principal itself not
150   much the worse. Away with't!

      HELENA   How might one do, sir, to lose it to her own lik-
        ing?

153 PAROLLES   Let me see. Marry, ill, to like him that ne'er it
154   likes. 'Tis a commodity will lose the gloss with lying:
155   the longer kept, the less worth. Off with't while 'tis
156   vendible; answer the time of request. Virginity, like an
157   old courtier, wears her cap out of fashion, richly suited,
158   but unsuitable, just like the brooch and the toothpick,

---

135 *stand for* defend; *die* (with possible pun on "experience orgasm") 137
in't in its behalf   138 *on the part of* in defense of   139 *infallible* undoubted
140 *is a virgin* i.e., is like a virgin (virginity being akin to suicide in that it results in the death of the continued life that offspring bring)   141–42 *out . . .
limit* in unconsecrated ground   143 *breeds mites* i.e., breeds its own destruc-
tion (like stale *cheese* breeds mold or worms)   144–45 *feeding . . . stomach*
maintaining its own pride   146 *inhibited* prohibited   147 *canon* catalogue
of sins   147 *Keep* hoard   148 *Out with't* lend out at interest; *make itself two*
increase twofold   149 *increase* rate of interest; *principal* capital (i.e., the former virgin herself)   153–54 *ill . . . likes* one must do ill, and like the man
who does not like virginity   154 *lying* lying idle   155 *Off with't* dispose of it
156 *answer . . . request* market it while it is still in demand   157 *out of fashion* unfashionably   157–58 *richly . . . unsuitable* dressed richly but inappro-
priately

which wear not now. Your date is better in your pie and   159
your porridge than in your cheek; and your virginity,   160
your old virginity, is like one of our French withered
pears: it looks ill, it eats drily. Marry, 'tis a withered pear;   162
it was formerly better; marry, yet 'tis a withered pear! Will
you anything with it?

HELENA

Not my virginity yet. . . .   165
There shall your master have a thousand loves,   166
A mother, and a mistress, and a friend,
A phoenix, captain, and an enemy,   168
A guide, a goddess, and a sovereign,
A counselor, a traitress, and a dear;   170
His humble ambition, proud humility,
His jarring concord, and his discord dulcet,   172
His faith, his sweet disaster; with a world
Of pretty, fond, adoptious christendoms   174
That blinking Cupid gossips. Now shall he –   175
I know not what he shall. God send him well!
The court's a learning place, and he is one –   177

PAROLLES

What one, i' faith?

HELENA   That I wish well. 'Tis pity –

PAROLLES

What's pity?

HELENA

That wishing well had not a body in't,   180

---

159 *wear not* are not worn   159–60 *Your . . . cheek* dates (fruit) serve better
to sweeten porridge than to show up (as years) in your face (i.e., as wrinkles)
162 *eats drily* tastes dry   165 *Not . . . yet* the moment has not come for me
to surrender my virginity (?) (there may be a segment of text missing here)
166 *There* at court (?)   166–73 *loves . . . disaster* (a series of epithets for the
beloved female common to much of Elizabethan love poetry)   168 *phoenix*
fabulous bird reputed to spring anew from its incineration   172 *dulcet* sweet
174 *fond . . . christendoms* foolish nicknames   175 *That . . . gossips* for which
blind Cupid (the god of love) acts as godfather (i.e., inspired by love)   177
learning place place of learning, school   180–81 *That . . . felt* that good will
were not something substantial, and in itself effective

181   Which might be felt; that we, the poorer born,
182   Whose baser stars do shut us up in wishes,
183   Might with effects of them follow our friends,
184   And show what we alone must think, which never
      Returns us thanks.
            Enter Page.
      PAGE   Monsieur Parolles, my lord calls for you.   *[Exit.]*
      PAROLLES   Little Helen, farewell. If I can remember thee,
      I will think of thee at court.
      HELENA   Monsieur Parolles, you were born under a char-
190   itable star.
191   PAROLLES   Under Mars I.
      HELENA   I especially think, under Mars.
      PAROLLES   Why under Mars?
194   HELENA   The wars hath so kept you under that you must
      needs be born under Mars.
196   PAROLLES   When he was predominant.
197   HELENA   When he was retrograde, I think rather.
      PAROLLES   Why think you so?
      HELENA   You go so much backward when you fight.
200   PAROLLES   That's for advantage.
      HELENA   So is running away when fear proposes the
202   safety. But the composition that your valor and fear
203   makes in you is a virtue of a good wing, and I like the
204   wear well.
205   PAROLLES   I am so full of businesses I cannot answer thee
206   acutely. I will return perfect courtier, in the which my

---

181 *poorer* non-nobly   **182** *Whose . . . wishes* whose inferior fortunes con-
fine us to mere wishing   **183** *Might . . . follow* might actively assist   **184–85**
show . . . thanks make manifest (in acts) what we must otherwise conceal in
our thoughts and so remain unthanked for   **191** *Under Mars* under the as-
trological influence of Mars, the Roman god of war   **194** *under* down   **196**
predominant in the ascendant   **197** *retrograde* unfavorably disposed, moving
apparently in a direction contrary to the order of the zodiac (i.e., going backward)   **200** *advantage* strategic benefit   **202** *composition* mixture   **203**
virtue property; *of . . . wing* useful for flight (especially from battle)   **204**
wear fashion   **205** *so . . . businesses* too preoccupied   **206** *acutely* aptly; *perfect* a complete

instruction shall serve to naturalize thee, so thou wilt   207
be capable of a courtier's counsel, and understand what   208
advice shall thrust upon thee; else thou diest in thine
unthankfulness, and thine ignorance makes thee away.   210
Farewell. When thou hast leisure, say thy prayers; when
thou hast none, remember thy friends. Get thee a good
husband, and use him as he uses thee. So, farewell.   213

                                                          [Exit.]

HELENA
Our remedies oft in ourselves do lie,
Which we ascribe to heaven. The fated sky   215
Gives us free scope; only doth backward pull
Our slow designs when we ourselves are dull.   217
What power is it which mounts my love so high?   218
That makes me see, and cannot feed mine eye?   219
The mightiest space in fortune nature brings   220
To join like likes, and kiss like native things.
Impossible be strange attempts to those
That weigh their pains in sense, and do suppose   223
What hath been cannot be. Who ever strove
To show her merit that did miss her love?   225
The king's disease – my project may deceive me,   226
But my intents are fixed, and will not leave me. *[Exit.]*
                                         *

---

207 *naturalize* familiarize, and, in Parolles' sense, deflower; *so* if   208 *capable* receptive, in a position to profit from (with sexual meaning, continued in *understand, thrust,* and *diest*)   210 *makes thee away* destroys you (Parolles returns to his claim that to be a virgin is equivalent to death)   213 *use* treat   215 *fated* fateful   217 *dull* sluggish, unenterprising   218 *so high* i.e., to one of Bertram's rank   219 *makes . . . eye* enables me to envisage Bertram in my mind's eye without allowing me to see him in the flesh   220–21 *The . . . things* nature causes things of the widest diversity in station to unite and embrace as though born equals   223 *That . . . sense* who count the cost and measure their discomforts   225 *miss* fail to achieve   226 *deceive* (1) fail, (2) mislead

⮾ **I.2** *Flourish cornets. Enter the King of France with letters, and divers Attendants.*

KING

1   The Florentines and Senoys are by th' ears,
     Have fought with equal fortune, and continue
3   A braving war.

FIRST LORD   So 'tis reported, sir.

KING

     Nay, 'tis most credible. We here receive it
5   A certainty vouched from our cousin Austria,
6   With caution, that the Florentine will move us
     For speedy aid; wherein our dearest friend
8   Prejudicates the business, and would seem
     To have us make denial.

FIRST LORD   His love and wisdom,
10   Approved so to your majesty, may plead
11   For amplest credence.

KING   He hath armed our answer,
     And Florence is denied before he comes.
13   Yet, for our gentlemen that mean to see
14   The Tuscan service, freely have they leave
15   To stand on either part.

SECOND LORD   It well may serve
16   A nursery to our gentry, who are sick
17   For breathing and exploit.

KING   What's he comes here?

     Enter Bertram, Lafew, and Parolles.

FIRST LORD

     It is the Count Rossillion, my good lord,
     Young Bertram.

KING   Youth, thou bear'st thy father's face.

I.2 Paris, the palace of the King of France   **1** *Senoys* Sienese; *by th' ears* at war
3 *braving* defiant   **5** *cousin* fellow monarch   **6** *move* petition   **8** *Prejudicates*
prejudges   **10** *Approved* proved   **11** *credence* credibility; *armed our answer*
i.e., strengthened our denial   **13** *for* as for; *see* experience   **14** *service* military service; *leave* permission   **15** *stand* serve; *part* side   **16** *nursery* training
ground; *are sick* crave   **17** *breathing* exercise

Frank nature, rather curious than in haste,   20
Hath well composed thee. Thy father's moral parts   21
Mayst thou inherit too! Welcome to Paris.

BERTRAM
My thanks and duty are your majesty's.

KING
I would I had that corporal soundness now   24
As when thy father and myself in friendship
First tried our soldiership. He did look far   26
Into the service of the time, and was   27
Discipled of the bravest. He lasted long,
But on us both did haggish age steal on,   29
And wore us out of act. It much repairs me   30
To talk of your good father; in his youth
He had the wit which I can well observe
Today in our young lords; but they may jest
Till their own scorn return to them unnoted   34
Ere they can hide their levity in honor.   35
So like a courtier, contempt nor bitterness   36
Were in his pride, or sharpness. If they were,
His equal had awaked them, and his honor,   38
Clock to itself, knew the true minute when   39
Exception bid him speak, and at this time   40
His tongue obeyed his hand. Who were below him   41
He used as creatures of another place,   42
And bowed his eminent top to their low ranks,
Making them proud of his humility,
In their poor praise he humbled. Such a man   45

---

20 *Frank* liberal; *curious* careful   21 *composed* constructed   24 *corporal* bodily   26–27 *did . . . time* deeply understood the business of war   27–28 *was . . . bravest* numbered the bravest among his followers   29 *haggish* haglike, ill-willed; *steal on* creep up on   30 *wore . . . act* reduced us to inaction; *repairs* restores   34 *unnoted* unnoticed   35 *hide . . . honor* cover their frivolity with truly honorable action   36 *contempt nor bitterness* neither contempt nor bitterness   38 *equal* social equal   39 *Clock to itself* self-regulating; *true* exact   40 *Exception* disapproval   41 *His . . . hand* he said only what the hand (i.e., of his clock of honor) prescribed; *Who* those who   42 *another place* i.e., a higher rank   45 *In . . . humbled* he graciously condescended to the humble by praising them (?)

Might be a copy to these younger times,
Which, followed well, would demonstrate them now
48   But goers backward.
BERTRAM   His good remembrance, sir,
Lies richer in your thoughts than on his tomb.
50   So in approof lives not his epitaph
As in your royal speech.
KING
Would I were with him! He would always say –
53   Methinks I hear him now; his plausive words
54   He scattered not in ears, but grafted them
To grow there, and to bear –"Let me not live"–
This his good melancholy oft began,
57   On the catastrophe and heel of pastime,
58   When it was out –"Let me not live," quoth he,
59   "After my flame lacks oil, to be the snuff
60   Of younger spirits, whose apprehensive senses
61   All but new things disdain; whose judgments are
Mere fathers of their garments; whose constancies
Expire before their fashions." This he wished.
I, after him, do after him wish too,
Since I nor wax nor honey can bring home,
66   I quickly were dissolvèd from my hive,
To give some laborers room.
SECOND LORD   You're loved, sir.
68   They that least lend it you shall lack you first.
KING
I fill a place, I know't. How long is't, count,
70   Since the physician at your father's died?

---

48 *goers backward* laggards   **50–51** *So . . . As* the tribute on his tomb is
nowhere better verified than   **53** *plausive* worthy of applause   **54**
scattered . . . grafted did not strew superficially among his hearers, but
planted deeply   **57** *catastrophe and heel* end and completion   **58** *it* i.e., *pastime*, l.57; *out* over   **59** *snuff* charred wicks impeding free burning, hence
hindrance, nuisance   **60** *apprehensive* keen   **61–62** *whose . . . garments*
whose minds are wholly taken up with devising new fashions   **66** *dissolvèd*
separated   **68** *lend it you* acknowledge it; *lack* miss

He was much famed.
BERTRAM   Some six months since, my lord.
KING
  If he were living, I would try him yet.
  Lend me an arm. The rest have worn me out
  With several applications; nature and sickness   74
  Debate it at their leisure. Welcome, count;   75
  My son's no dearer.
BERTRAM   Thank your majesty.
                                   Exeunt. Flourish.

                            ✳

∾ **I.3** *Enter Countess, Steward, and [Lavatch, a] Clown.*

COUNTESS   I will now hear. What say you of this gentlewoman?
STEWARD   Madam, the care I have had to even your con-   3
  tent I wish might be found in the calendar of my past   4
  endeavors; for then we wound our modesty, and make
  foul the clearness of our deservings, when of ourselves 6
  we publish them.   7
COUNTESS   What does this knave here? *[To Lavatch]* Get
  you gone, sirrah. The complaints I have heard of you I
  do not all believe. 'Tis my slowness that I do not; for I   10
  know you lack not folly to commit them, and have
  ability enough to make such knaveries yours.
LAVATCH   'Tis not unknown to you, madam, I am a poor
  fellow.
COUNTESS   Well, sir.   15
LAVATCH   No, madam, 'tis not so well that I am poor,
  though many of the rich are damned; but if I may have

---

74 *several applications* various treatments   75 *Debate . . . leisure* contend at
length
    I.3 The palace of the Countess of Rossillion   3–4 *even your content* satisfy
your wishes   4–5 *calendar . . . endeavors* record of my past service   6 *clearness* luster; *deservings* deserts   7 *publish* make known   15 *Well* and so, what
of it

18   your ladyship's good will to go to the world, Isbel the
      woman and I will do as we may.
20 COUNTESS   Wilt thou needs be a beggar?
   LAVATCH   I do beg your good will in this case.
   COUNTESS   In what case?
23 LAVATCH   In Isbel's case and mine own. Service is no her-
      itage, and I think I shall never have the blessing of God
25   till I have issue o' my body; for they say barnes are
      blessings.
   COUNTESS   Tell me thy reason why thou wilt marry.
   LAVATCH   My poor body, madam, requires it; I am
      driven on by the flesh; and he must needs go that the
30   devil drives.
   COUNTESS   Is this all your worship's reason?
   LAVATCH   Faith, madam, I have other holy reasons, such
      as they are.
   COUNTESS   May the world know them?
   LAVATCH   I have been, madam, a wicked creature, as you
      and all flesh and blood are, and indeed I do marry that
      I may repent.
   COUNTESS   Thy marriage, sooner than thy wickedness.
39 LAVATCH   I am out o' friends, madam, and I hope to
40   have friends for my wife's sake.
   COUNTESS   Such friends are thine enemies, knave.
42 LAVATCH   You're shallow, madam, in great friends; for the
43   knaves come to do that for me which I am aweary of.
44   He that ears my land spares my team and gives me leave
45   to in the crop; if I be his cuckold, he's my drudge. He
      that comforts my wife is the cherisher of my flesh and
      blood; he that cherishes my flesh and blood loves my
      flesh and blood; he that loves my flesh and blood is my
      friend: ergo, he that kisses my wife is my friend. If men
50   could be contented to be what they are, there were no

18 *go . . . world* get married   23 *case* (slang for vagina); *Service* i.e., being a
servant   23–24 *heritage* lineage ("Service is no heritage" is a proverb, as are
many of Lavatch's remarks)   25 *barnes* children   39 *out o'* without   42
shallow . . . in superficial . . . in judging   43 *that* i.e., sexual service   44 *ears*
plows   45 *in* harvest   50 *what they are* i.e., cuckolds

fear in marriage; for young Charbon the puritan and   51
old Poysam the papist, howsome'er their hearts are sev-   52
ered in religion, their heads are both one – they may   53
jowl horns together like any deer i' th' herd.   54

COUNTESS   Wilt thou ever be a foulmouthed and calum-
nious knave?

LAVATCH   A prophet I, madam, and I speak the truth the
next way: 58

        For I the ballad will repeat,
           Which men full true shall find: 60
        Your marriage comes by destiny,
           Your cuckoo sings by kind.   62

COUNTESS   Get you gone, sir. I'll talk with you more
anon.

STEWARD   May it please you, madam, that he bid Helen
come to you. Of her I am to speak.

COUNTESS   Sirrah, tell my gentlewoman I would speak
with her – Helen I mean.

LAVATCH

        "Was this fair face the cause," quoth she,   69
           "Why the Grecians sackèd Troy?   70
        Fond done, done fond,   71
           Was this King Priam's joy?"   72
        With that she sighèd as she stood,
        With that she sighèd as she stood,
           And gave this sentence then:
        "Among nine bad if one be good,
        Among nine bad if one be good,
           There's yet one good in ten."

COUNTESS   What, one good in ten? You corrupt the   79
song, sirrah.   80

---

51 *Charbon* (French *chair bonne* – i.e., meat eater)   52 *Poysam* (French *pois-son* – i.e., fish eater)   52–53 *severed* divided   53 *both one* exactly alike   54 *jowl* knock; *deer . . . herd* horned beasts (i.e., cuckolds)   58 *next* nearest   62 *kind* nature   69 *she* (possibly Hecuba, widow of Priam)   71 *Fond* foolishly (with pun on "caressingly")   72 *Priam* king of Troy   79–80 *corrupt the song* (the original song presumably found one "bad" in ten; the clown reverses the proportions)

LAVATCH   One good woman in ten, madam, which is a
purifying o' th' song. Would God would serve the
83   world so all the year! We'd find no fault with the tithe
84   woman, if I were the parson. One in ten, quoth a? An
85   we might have a good woman born but or every blaz-
86   ing star, or at an earthquake, 'twould mend the lottery
87   well; a man may draw his heart out ere a pluck one.

COUNTESS   You'll be gone, sir knave, and do as I command you.

90   LAVATCH   That man should be at woman's command,
91   and yet no hurt done! Though honesty be no puritan,
92   yet it will do no hurt; it will wear the surplice of humility over the black gown of a big heart. I am going, for-
sooth. The business is for Helen to come hither.   *Exit.*

COUNTESS   Well now.

STEWARD   I know, madam, you love your gentlewoman
entirely.

98   COUNTESS   Faith, I do. Her father bequeathed her to me,
99   and she herself, without other advantage, may lawfully
100   make title to as much love as she finds. There is more
owing her than is paid, and more shall be paid her than
she'll demand.

STEWARD   Madam, I was very late more near her than I
think she wished me; alone she was, and did communi-
cate to herself her own words to her own ears. She
106   thought, I dare vow for her, they touched not any

83–84 *We'd . . . parson* one good woman in ten (*tithe woman* – i.e., tenth woman) ought to satisfy the parson as well as one pig in ten (the traditional contribution to support the parish minister)   **84** *a* he; *An* if   **85–86** *or . . . or* either . . . or; *blazing star* new star or comet   **86** *mend the lottery* improve the existing odds   **87** *a pluck one* he draws a good woman (in the lottery of marriage)   **91** *honesty* chastity   **92–93** *wear . . . heart* conform to ecclesiasti-cal rules by wearing the *surplice* (the state-sanctioned costume of prelacy), but remain inwardly rebellious (with a prideful, or *big*, heart) by wearing the unadorned black gown of the sectarians underneath   **98** *bequeathed . . . me* entrusted, named me as her guardian   **99** *without other advantage* other claims apart   **100** *make title to* claim   **106–7** *touched . . . sense* could not be overheard

stranger sense. Her matter was, she loved your son. Fortune, she said, was no goddess, that had put such dif-
ference betwixt their two estates; Love no god, that
would not extend his might, only where qualities were   110
level; [Diana no] queen of virgins, that would suffer her
poor knight surprised without rescue in the first as-   112
sault, or ransom afterward. This she delivered in the
most bitter touch of sorrow that e'er I heard virgin ex-   114
claim in, which I held my duty speedily to acquaint
you withal, sithence, in the loss that may happen, it   116
concerns you something to know it.   117

COUNTESS You have discharged this honestly; keep it to
yourself. Many likelihoods informed me of this before,   119
which hung so tottering in the balance that I could nei-   120
ther believe nor misdoubt. Pray you leave me; stall this   121
in your bosom; and I thank you for your honest care. I
will speak with you further anon.   *Exit Steward.*
    Enter Helena.
Even so it was with me when I was young.
    If ever we are nature's, these are ours. This thorn   125
Doth to our rose of youth rightly belong;
    Our blood to us, this to our blood is born.   127
It is the show and seal of nature's truth,   128
Where love's strong passion is impressed in youth.
By our remembrances of days foregone,   130
Such were our faults, or then we thought them none.   131
Her eye is sick on't; I observe her now.   132

HELENA
    What is your pleasure, madam?
COUNTESS   You know, Helen,

110–11 *qualities were level* social rank was equal   112 *knight* i.e., follower
(Helena)   114 *touch* note   116 *withal* with; *sithence* since; *loss* i.e., (1) of
Helena's virginity, (2) of Bertram's family honor   117 *something* somewhat
119 *likelihoods* signs   121 *stall* lodge   125 *these* i.e., pangs of love   127
blood natural instincts   128 *show . . . truth* sign and certificate of the gen-
uineness of our human nature   131 *or . . . none* or, rather, in those days we
did not think them faults   132 *on't* with it

I am a mother to you.

HELENA
Mine honorable mistress.

COUNTESS   Nay, a mother.
Why not a mother? When I said "a mother,"
Methought you saw a serpent. What's in "mother"
That you start at it? I say I am your mother,
And put you in the catalogue of those
140   That were enwombèd mine. 'Tis often seen
141   Adoption strives with nature, and choice breeds
A native slip to us from foreign seeds.
You ne'er oppressed me with a mother's groan,
Yet I express to you a mother's care.
God's mercy, maiden, does it curd thy blood
To say I am thy mother? What's the matter,
147   That this distemperèd messenger of wet,
148   The many-colored Iris, rounds thine eye?
Why? that you are my daughter?

HELENA   That I am not.

COUNTESS
150   I say I am your mother.

HELENA   Pardon, madam.
The Count Rossillion cannot be my brother:
I am from humble, he from honorèd name;
153   No note upon my parents, his all noble.
My master, my dear lord he is, and I
His servant live and will his vassal die.
He must not be my brother.

COUNTESS   Nor I your mother?

HELENA
You are my mother, madam. Would you were –
So that my lord your son were not my brother –

---

141 *strives* competes in strength of love   141–42 *choice . . . seeds* by adoption we make wholly our own what was originally foreign   147 *distemperèd*
disordered; *messenger of wet* tear   148 *Iris* rainbow; *rounds* encircles   153
note mark of distinction; *parents* kinsmen

Indeed my mother! or were you both our mothers,   159
I care no more for than I do for heaven,   *160*
So I were not his sister. Can't no other,   161
But I your daughter, he must be my brother?
COUNTESS
Yes, Helen, you might be my daughter-in-law.
God shield you mean it not! "daughter" and "mother"   164
So strive upon your pulse. What, pale again?
My fear hath catched your fondness. Now I see   166
The myst'ry of your loneliness, and find
Your salt tears' head. Now to all sense 'tis gross: 168
You love my son. Invention is ashamed,   169
Against the proclamation of thy passion,   170
To say thou dost not. Therefore tell me true;
But tell me then, 'tis so; for look, thy cheeks
Confess it, t' one to th' other, and thine eyes
See it so grossly shown in thy behaviors   174
That in their kind they speak it. Only sin   175
And hellish obstinacy tie thy tongue,
That truth should be suspected. Speak, is't so?   177
If it be so, you have wound a goodly clew;   178
If it be not, forswear't; howe'er, I charge thee,   179
As heaven shall work in me for thine avail,   180
To tell me truly.
HELENA   Good madam, pardon me.
COUNTESS
Do you love my son?
HELENA   Your pardon, noble mistress!

---

159 *both our mothers* mother of us both   **161–62** *Can't . . . But* can it be no
other way than if   **164** *shield* forbid   **166** *fondness* foolishness and/or love
(for Bertram)   **168** *head* source; *gross* evident   **169** *Invention* fabrication of
excuses   **170** *Against* in the face of   **174** *grossly* openly   **175** *in their kind*
after their nature (i.e., by weeping)   **177** *That . . . suspected* that the truth
must be guessed at rather than plainly declared, as it ought to be   **178**
wound . . . clew snarled things up handsomely   **179** *forswear't* deny it   **180**
avail benefit

COUNTESS
Love you my son?

HELENA   Do not you love him, madam?

COUNTESS
184 Go not about; my love hath in't a bond
Whereof the world takes note. Come, come, disclose
The state of your affection, for your passions
187 Have to the full appeached.

HELENA   *[Kneels.]*   Then I confess
Here on my knee before high heaven and you,
That before you, and next unto high heaven,
190 I love your son.
191 My friends were poor but honest; so's my love.
Be not offended, for it hurts not him
That he is loved of me. I follow him not
194 By any token of presumptuous suit,
Nor would I have him till I do deserve him;
Yet never know how that desert should be.
I know I love in vain, strive against hope;
198 Yet in this captious and intenible sieve
199 I still pour in the waters of my love
200 And lack not to lose still. Thus, Indian-like,
Religious in mine error, I adore
The sun that looks upon his worshiper
But knows of him no more. My dearest madam,
204 Let not your hate encounter with my love,
For loving where you do; but if yourself,
206 Whose agèd honor cites a virtuous youth,
Did ever in so true a flame of liking,
208 Wish chastely and love dearly, that your Dian
209 Was both herself and Love, O, then give pity

---

184 *Go not about* don't beat about the bush   187 *appeached* informed
against you   191 *friends* relations   194 *presumptuous suit* overambitious
wooing   198 *captious* (1) capacious, (2) deceptive; *intenible* unretentive
199 *still* constantly   200 *lack . . . still* have enough to continue pouring out
and losing indefinitely; *Indian-like* idolatrously   204 *encounter with* oppose
itself to   206 *cites* betokens   208 *that* so that   209 *both . . . Love* i.e., both
chaste and passionate

To her whose state is such that cannot choose   *210*
But lend and give where she is sure to lose;
That seeks not to find that her search implies,   *212*
But, riddlelike, lives sweetly where she dies.   *213*

COUNTESS
Had you not lately an intent – speak truly –
To go to Paris?

HELENA   Madam, I had.

COUNTESS   Wherefore? Tell true.

HELENA
I will tell truth, by grace itself I swear:
You know my father left me some prescriptions
Of rare and proved effects, such as his reading
And manifest experience had collected
For general sovereignty; and that he willed me   *220*
In heedful'st reservation to bestow them,   *221*
As notes whose faculties inclusive were   *222*
More than they were in note. Amongst the rest
There is a remedy, approved, set down,   *224*
To cure the desperate languishings whereof
The king is rendered lost.   *226*

COUNTESS   This was your motive
For Paris, was it? Speak.

HELENA
My lord your son made me to think of this;
Else Paris, and the medicine, and the king
Had from the conversation of my thoughts   *230*
Happily been absent then.   *231*

COUNTESS   But think you, Helen,
If you should tender your supposèd aid,   *232*
He would receive it? He and his physicians
Are of a mind: he, that they cannot help him;
They, that they cannot help. How shall they credit

---

212 *that* what   213 *riddlelike* paradoxically   220 *For general sovereignty* as
master remedies   221 *In . . . them* to reserve them carefully for special uses
222–23 *As . . . note* as prescriptions more potent than generally recognized
224 *approved* tested   226 *rendered lost* given up as incurable   230 *conversa-tion* interchange   231 *Happily* haply, perchance   232 *tender* offer

236 A poor unlearnèd virgin, when the schools,
237 Emboweled of their doctrine, have left off
    The danger to itself?
HELENA   There's something in't
    More than my father's skill, which was the great'st
240 Of his profession, that his good receipt
    Shall for my legacy be sanctified
    By th' luckiest stars in heaven; and would your honor
    But give me leave to try success, I'd venture
244 The well-lost life of mine on his grace's cure
    By such a day and hour.
COUNTESS   Dost thou believe't?
HELENA
246 Ay, madam, knowingly.
COUNTESS
    Why, Helen, thou shalt have my leave and love,
    Means and attendants, and my loving greetings
    To those of mine in court. I'll stay at home
250 And pray God's blessing into thy attempt.
    Be gone tomorrow, and be sure of this,
    What I can help thee to, thou shalt not miss.   *Exeunt.*

*

∾ **II.1** *Enter the King with divers young Lords taking
leave for the Florentine war; [Bertram] Count
Rossillion, and Parolles. Flourish cornets.*

KING
    Farewell, young lords; these warlike principles
2 Do not throw from you. And you, my lords, farewell.
3 Share the advice betwixt you; if both gain all,

---

236 *schools* medical faculties   237 *Emboweled . . . doctrine* depleted of their
knowledge   237–38 *left . . . itself* abandoned the disease to its course   240
that whereby; *receipt* prescription   244 *well-lost* i.e., in such a cause   246
knowingly with full knowledge
    II.1 The palace of the King of France   2 *throw from you* abandon   3–5
if . . . for both if both groups of you follow my advice, my gift will be that
much ampler, and will serve for both

The gift doth stretch itself as 'tis received,
And is enough for both.
FIRST LORD   'Tis our hope, sir,
    After well-entered soldiers, to return   6
    And find your grace in health.
KING
    No, no, it cannot be. And yet my heart
    Will not confess he owes the malady   9
    That doth my life besiege. Farewell, young lords.   10
    Whether I live or die, be you the sons
    Of worthy Frenchmen. Let Higher Italy
    (Those bated that inherit but the fall   13
    Of the last monarchy) see that you come
    Not to woo honor, but to wed it, when   15
    The bravest questant shrinks: find what you seek,   16
    That fame may cry you loud. I say, farewell.   17
SECOND LORD
    Health at your bidding serve your majesty!
KING
    Those girls of Italy, take heed of them.
    They say our French lack language to deny   20
    If they demand; beware of being captives   21
    Before you serve.
BOTH   Our hearts receive your warnings.
KING
    Farewell. *[To Attendants]* Come hither to me.
                            [Exit, led by Attendants.]
FIRST LORD
    O, my sweet lord, that you will stay behind us!
PAROLLES
    'Tis not his fault, the spark.   25
SECOND LORD   O, 'tis brave wars!

---

6 *After . . . soldiers* after making a worthy debut as soldiers 9 *owes* owns 13 *Those . . . but* except for those responsible for 15 *woo* i.e., flirt with; *wed* possess 16 *questant* seeker 17 *cry* proclaim 21 *captives* i.e., to love 25 *spark* elegant young man; *brave* wonderful, valiant

PAROLLES
    Most admirable. I have seen those wars.
27 BERTRAM   I am commanded here and kept a coil with
    "Too young," and "The next year," and "'Tis too early."
29 PAROLLES   An thy mind stand to't, boy, steal away
30   bravely.
    BERTRAM
31   I shall stay here the forehorse to a smock,
32   Creaking my shoes on the plain masonry,
33   Till honor be bought up, and no sword worn
    But one to dance with. By heaven, I'll steal away!
    FIRST LORD
    There's honor in the theft.
    PAROLLES   Commit it, count.
    SECOND LORD
    I am your accessory; and so farewell.
37 BERTRAM   I grow to you, and our parting is a tortured
    body.
    FIRST LORD   Farewell, captain.
40 SECOND LORD   Sweet Monsieur Parolles!
    PAROLLES   Noble heroes, my sword and yours are kin.
42   Good sparks and lustrous, a word, good metals: you
    shall find in the regiment of the Spinii one Captain
44   Spurio, with his cicatrix, an emblem of war, here on his
45   sinister cheek. It was this very sword entrenched it; say
    to him I live, and observe his reports for me.
    FIRST LORD   We shall, noble captain.
48 PAROLLES   Mars dote on you for his novices!
                                          [Exeunt Lords.]
    What will ye do?
        [Enter the King, led back to his chair by Attendants.]
50 BERTRAM   Stay – the king.

---

27 *kept a coil* fussed over   29 *An* if   30 *bravely* valiantly   31 *forehorse* leading
horse; *smock* woman   32 *plain masonry* level palace floors (instead of the
rough battlefield)   33 *Till . . . up* till the supply of honor is exhausted   37
grow to grow deeply attached to   37–38 *a tortured body* like a body being torn
apart   42 *metals* (with pun on "mettles")   44 *cicatrix* scar   45 *sinister* left
48 *Mars . . . novices* may Mars favor you as his newest votaries

PAROLLES   Use a more spacious ceremony to the noble 51
  lords, you have restrained yourself within the list of too 52
  cold an adieu. Be more expressive to them; for they 53
  wear themselves in the cap of the time; there do muster 54
  true gait, eat, speak, and move under the influence of 55
  the most received star; and though the devil lead the
  measure, such are to be followed. After them, and take 57
  a more dilated farewell. 58

BERTRAM   And I will do so.

PAROLLES   Worthy fellows, and like to prove most sinewy 60
  swordmen.   *Exeunt [Bertram and Parolles].*
       Enter Lafew.

LAFEW *[Kneels.]*
  Pardon, my lord, for me and for my tidings.

KING
  I'll fee thee to stand up. 63

LAFEW *[Rises.]*
  Then here's a man stands that has brought his pardon.
  I would you had kneeled, my lord, to ask me mercy,
  And that at my bidding you could so stand up.

KING
  I would I had, so I had broke thy pate
  And asked thee mercy for't. 68

LAFEW   Good faith, across!
  But, my good lord, 'tis thus: will you be cured
  Of your infirmity? 70

KING   No.

LAFEW   O, will you eat
  No grapes, my royal fox? Yes, but you will 71
  My noble grapes, an if my royal fox 72
  Could reach them. I have seen a medicine

---

51 *spacious* elaborate 52 *list* bounds 53 *expressive* unreserved 54
wear . . . time shine in the fashionable world 54–55 *muster true gait* set the
right pace 55–56 *move . . . star* conform to the reigning fashions 57 *measure* dance; *such* such leaders 58 *dilated* extended 63 *fee* pay 68 *across*
wide of the mark (referring to the king's attempt at a jest in ll. 67–68) 71
fox (in Aesop's *Fables,* the fox disdained as sour the grapes that were beyond
his reach)

That's able to breathe life into a stone,
75 Quicken a rock, and make you dance canary
With sprightly fire and motion; whose simple touch
77 Is powerful to araise King Pepin, nay,
To give great Charlemagne a pen in's hand,
And write to her a love line.

KING   What "her" is this?

LAFEW
80 Why, Doctor She! My lord, there's one arrived,
If you will see her. Now by my faith and honor,
If seriously I may convey my thoughts
83 In this my light deliverance, I have spoke
84 With one that in her sex, her years, profession,
85 Wisdom and constancy, hath amazed me more
Than I dare blame my weakness. Will you see her,
For that is her demand, and know her business?
That done, laugh well at me.

KING   Now, good Lafew,
89 Bring in the admiration, that we with thee
90 May spend our wonder too, or take off thine
91 By wond'ring how thou took'st it.

LAFEW   Nay, I'll fit you,
And not be all day neither.   *[Exit.]*

KING
93 Thus he his special nothing ever prologues.
    Enter [Lafew, with] Helena.

LAFEW
94 Nay, come your ways.

KING   This haste hath wings indeed.

LAFEW
Nay, come your ways;
This is his majesty; say your mind to him.

---

75 *Quicken* bring to life; *canary* a lively Spanish dance   77 *araise* raise up;
King Pepin an eighth-century Frankish king, father of Charlemagne   83 *light
deliverance* frivolous delivery   84 *profession* claim   85–86 *more . . . weakness*
more than I can account for by blaming my senility   89 *admiration* wonder
90 *spend* utter; *take off* dispel, remove   91 *took'st* came by; *fit* satisfy   93 *special nothing* particular trifles   94 *your ways* along

A traitor you do look like, but such traitors   97
His majesty seldom fears. I am Cressid's uncle,   98
That dare leave two together. Fare you well.   *Exit.*

KING
Now, fair one, does your business follow us?   100

HELENA
Ay, my good lord.
Gerard de Narbon was my father;
In what he did profess, well-found.   103

KING   I knew him.

HELENA
The rather will I spare my praises towards him;
Knowing him is enough. On's bed of death
Many receipts he gave me, chiefly one,   106
Which as the dearest issue of his practice   107
And of his old experience th' only darling,   108
He bade me store up as a triple eye,   109
Safer than mine own two, more dear; I have so;   *110*
And hearing your high majesty is touched
With that malignant cause wherein the honor   112
Of my dear father's gift stands chief in power,
I come to tender it and my appliance,   114
With all bound humbleness.   115

KING   We thank you, maiden;
But may not be so credulous of cure,
When our most learnèd doctors leave us, and   117
The congregated college have concluded   118
That laboring art can never ransom nature   119
From her inaidable estate. I say we must not   120

---

97 *traitor . . . like* (because Helena's eyes are modestly cast down) 98 *Cressid's uncle* Pandarus (hence pander, who brought the lovers Troilus and Cressida together) 100 *follow* concern 103 *In . . . well-found* found to be good at his profession, medicine 106 *receipts* prescriptions 107 *dearest issue* most treasured product 108 *of . . . darling* the most cherished treasure of his ripest professional skill 109 *triple* third 112 *cause* disease 112–13 *wherein . . . power* for which my father's remedy is most effective 114 *tender* offer; *appliance* treatment 115 *bound* dutiful 117 *leave* give up for dead 118 *congregated college* conclave of physicians 119 *art* medicine 120 *inaidable estate* condition of hopelessness

121   So stain our judgment, or corrupt our hope,
       To prostitute our past-cure malady
123   To empirics, or to dissever so
124   Our great self and our credit, to esteem
125   A senseless help, when help past sense we deem.

HELENA
       My duty then shall pay me for my pains.
127   I will no more enforce mine office on you,
       Humbly entreating from your royal thoughts
129   A modest one, to bear me back again.

KING
130   I cannot give thee less, to be called grateful.
       Thou thought'st to help me, and such thanks I give
       As one near death to those that wish him live.
       But what at full I know, thou know'st no part,
       I knowing all my peril, thou no art.

HELENA
       What I can do can do no hurt to try,
136   Since you set up your rest 'gainst remedy.
       He that of greatest works is finisher
       Oft does them by the weakest minister.
       So holy writ in babes hath judgment shown
140   When judges have been babes; great floods have flown
141   From simple sources, and great seas have dried
       When miracles have by the greatest been denied.
143   Oft expectation fails, and most oft there
144   Where most it promises; and oft it hits
       Where hope is coldest and despair most shifts.

KING
       I must not hear thee; fare thee well, kind maid.
       Thy pains, not used, must by thyself be paid;

---

121 *corrupt our hope* hope foolishly   123 *empirics* quacks   123–24 *dissever . . . credit* divorce our greatness from our reputation (i.e., behave in an unkingly manner)   124 *esteem* value   125 *senseless* irrational; *past sense* unreasonable   127 *office* function   129 *A modest one* a belief in my good intentions and natural modesty   136 *set . . . rest* are resolved at all cost   140 *babes* i.e., helpless, foolish   141 *simple* insignificant   143 *expectation* that which we most confidently anticipate   144 *hits* succeeds

Proffers not took reap thanks for their reward.   148
HELENA
Inspirèd merit so by breath is barred.   149
It is not so with him that all things knows   150
As 'tis with us that square our guess by shows;   151
But most it is presumption in us, when
The help of heaven we count the act of men.
Dear sir, to my endeavors give consent;
Of heaven, not me, make an experiment.
I am not an impostor, that proclaim   156
Myself against the level of mine aim;
But know I think, and think I know most sure,
My art is not past power, nor you past cure.   159
KING
Art thou so confident? Within what space   *160*
Hop'st thou my cure?
HELENA   The great'st grace lending grace,
Ere twice the horses of the sun shall bring
Their fiery torcher his diurnal ring,   163
Ere twice in murk and occidental damp   164
Moist Hesperus hath quenched her sleepy lamp,   165
Or four and twenty times the pilot's glass   166
Hath told the thievish minutes how they pass,
What is infirm from your sound parts shall fly,
Health shall live free, and sickness freely die.
KING
Upon thy certainty and confidence   *170*
What dar'st thou venture?   171
HELENA   Tax of impudence,
A strumpet's boldness, a divulgèd shame   172

---

148 *thanks* i.e., only thanks   149 *Inspirèd* divinely inspired; *so* thus; *breath* words   150 *him* i.e., God   151 *square . . . shows* rule our opinions by appearances   156–57 *that . . . aim* who boasts of what he has yet to achieve   159 *past* beyond   163–66 (Helena seems to be promising two different schedules: forty-eight or twenty-four hours)   163 *torcher* torchbearer; *diurnal ring* daily round   164 *occidental* of sunset   165 *Hesperus* evening star; *her* (since the evening star is in fact the planet Venus)   166 *glass* hourglass   171 *Tax* charge   172 *divulgèd* publicly proclaimed

Traduced by odious ballads; my maiden's name
174   Seared otherwise; nay, worse of worst, extended
With vilest torture let my life be ended.

KING

Methinks in thee some blessèd spirit doth speak
177   His powerful sound within an organ weak;
178   And what impossibility would slay
In common sense, sense saves another way.
180   Thy life is dear, for all that life can rate
181   Worth name of life in thee hath estimate:
Youth, beauty, wisdom, courage – all
183   That happiness and prime can happy call.
184   Thou this to hazard needs must intimate
185   Skill infinite, or monstrous desperate.
186   Sweet practicer, thy physic I will try,
187   That ministers thine own death if I die.

HELENA

188   If I break time or flinch in property
Of what I spoke, unpitied let me die,
190   And well deserved; not helping, death's my fee.
But if I help, what do you promise me?

KING

192   Make thy demand.

HELENA   But will you make it even?

KING

Ay, by my scepter and my hopes of heaven.

HELENA

Then shalt thou give me with thy kingly hand
What husband in thy power I will command.
Exempted be from me the arrogance
To choose from forth the royal blood of France,

---

174 *otherwise* in other ways as well; *extended* stretched out, racked   177 *organ* instrument   178–79 *what . . . way* what common sense would regard as impossible, a higher sense can believe   181 *estimate* value   183 *prime* youth   184 *hazard* risk; *intimate* suggest   185 *monstrous desperate* extremely reckless   186 *practicer* practitioner; *physic* medicine   187 *ministers* administers   188 *break time* fail to perform in the stipulated time; *flinch in property* fall short in the particulars   192 *make it even* match it

My low and humble name to propagate
With any branch or image of thy state;
But such a one, thy vassal, whom I know   *200*
Is free for me to ask, thee to bestow.

KING
Here is my hand. The premises observed,
Thy will by my performance shall be served.
So make the choice of thy own time; for I,
Thy resolved patient, on thee still rely.   205
More should I question thee, and more I must,
Though more to know could not be more to trust –
From whence thou cam'st, how tended on – but rest   208
Unquestioned welcome, and undoubted blessed.
Give me some help here, ho! – If thou proceed   *210*
As high as word, my deed shall match thy deed.   211

                              Flourish. Exeunt.

                    *

∾ **II.2** *Enter Countess and [Lavatch, the] Clown.*

COUNTESS   Come on, sir, I shall now put you to the   1
    height of your breeding.
LAVATCH   I will show myself highly fed and lowly taught.   3
    I know my business is but to the court.
COUNTESS   To the court? Why, what place make you   5
    special, when you put off that with such contempt? But   6
    to the court?
LAVATCH   Truly, madam, if God have lent a man any
    manners, he may easily put it off at court: he that can-
    not make a leg, put off's cap, kiss his hand, and say   10
    nothing, has neither leg, hands, lip, nor cap; and in-
    deed such a fellow, to say precisely, were not for the
    court. But for me, I have an answer will serve all men.

---

205 *still* always   208 *tended on* attended   211 *word* promised
    II.2 The palace of the Countess of Rossillion   1–2 *put . . . height* test the
extent   3 *highly . . . taught* i.e., like a rich man's son, overfed and underdisci-
plined   5 *make* consider   6 *put off* dismiss   10 *leg* respectful bow

COUNTESS   Marry, that's a bountiful answer that fits all questions.

LAVATCH   It is like a barber's chair that fits all buttocks –
17   the pin buttock, the quatch buttock, the brawn buttock, or any buttock.

COUNTESS   Will your answer serve fit to all questions?

20   LAVATCH   As fit as ten groats is for the hand of an attor-
21   ney, as your French crown for your taffety punk, as
22   Tib's rush for Tom's forefinger, as a pancake for Shrove
23   Tuesday, a morris for May Day, as the nail to his hole,
24   the cuckold to his horn, as a scolding quean to a wran-
gling knave, as the nun's lip to the friar's mouth; nay, as
26   the pudding to his skin.

COUNTESS   Have you, I say, an answer of such fitness for all questions?

LAVATCH   From below your duke to beneath your con-
30   stable, it will fit any question.

COUNTESS   It must be an answer of most monstrous size that must fit all demands.

33   LAVATCH   But a trifle neither, in good faith, if the learned should speak truth of it. Here it is, and all that belongs to't: ask me if I am a courtier; it shall do you no harm to learn.

COUNTESS   To be young again, if we could! I will be a fool in question, hoping to be the wiser by your answer. I pray you, sir, are you a courtier?

40   LAVATCH   O Lord, sir! – There's a simple putting off. More, more, a hundred of them.

COUNTESS   Sir, I am a poor friend of yours, that loves you.

43   LAVATCH   O Lord, sir! – Thick, thick, spare not me.

COUNTESS   I think, sir, you can eat none of this homely meat.

LAVATCH   O Lord, sir! – Nay, put me to't, I warrant you.
COUNTESS   You were lately whipped, sir, as I think.
LAVATCH   O Lord, sir! – Spare not me.
COUNTESS   Do you cry "O Lord, sir!" at your whipping,
and "Spare not me"? Indeed, your "O Lord, sir!" is very   50
sequent to your whipping; you would answer very well   51
to a whipping, if you were but bound to't.   52
LAVATCH   I ne'er had worse luck in my life in my "O Lord,
sir!" I see things may serve long, but not serve ever.
COUNTESS
I play the noble housewife with the time,   55
To entertain it so merrily with a fool.
LAVATCH   O Lord, sir! – Why, there't serves well again.
COUNTESS
An end, sir! To your business: give Helen this,
And urge her to a present answer back.   59
Commend me to my kinsmen and my son.   60
This is not much.
LAVATCH   Not much commendation to them?
COUNTESS   Not much employment for you. You under-
stand me?
LAVATCH   Most fruitfully. I am there before my legs.   65
COUNTESS   Haste you again.   *Exeunt.*   66

*

❧ **II.3**   *Enter Count [Bertram], Lafew, and Parolles.*

LAFEW   They say miracles are past, and we have our   1
philosophical persons, to make modern and familiar,   2
things supernatural and causeless. Hence is it that we   3

50–51 *is . . . to* follows closely upon   51–52 *answer . . . to* repay (with pun
on "reply")   52 *bound* engaged (with pun on "tied up")   55 *noble housewife*
i.e., lady of leisure   59 *a present* an immediate   65 *fruitfully* abundantly
66 *again* back again

II.3 The royal court   1 *miracles are past* (Protestants believed that miracles ceased with Christ's ascent into heaven; Roman Catholics believed modern miracles possible)   2 *modern* commonplace   3 *causeless* of unknown
cause

4   make trifles of terrors, ensconcing ourselves into seem-
      ing knowledge when we should submit ourselves to an
6   unknown fear.
7   PAROLLES   Why, 'tis the rarest argument of wonder that
8   hath shot out in our latter times.
      BERTRAM   And so 'tis.
10   LAFEW   To be relinquished of the artists –
11   PAROLLES   So I say – both of Galen and Paracelsus –
12   LAFEW   Of all the learned and authentic fellows –
      PAROLLES   Right! So I say.
      LAFEW   That gave him out incurable –
      PAROLLES   Why, there 'tis! so say I too.
      LAFEW   Not to be helped –
      PAROLLES   Right! as 'twere a man assured of a –
      LAFEW   Uncertain life, and sure death.
      PAROLLES   Just! you say well. So would I have said.
20   LAFEW   I may truly say it is a novelty to the world.
21   PAROLLES   It is indeed. If you will have it in showing, you
      shall read it in What-do-ye-call there.   *[Indicates a*
      paper in Lafew's possession.]
23   LAFEW   *[Reads.]* "A showing of a heavenly effect in an
      earthly actor."
      PAROLLES   That's it I would have said, the very same.
26   LAFEW   Why, your dolphin is not lustier. 'Fore me, I
27   speak in respect –
      PAROLLES   Nay, 'tis strange, 'tis very strange! that is the
29   brief and the tedious of it; and he's of a most facineri-
30   ous spirit that will not acknowledge it to be the –

4–5 *ensconcing . . . knowledge* barricading ourselves within apparent knowledge   6 *unknown fear* fear of the unknown   7 *argument* theme   8 *shot out*
suddenly appeared (like a comet, believed to presage mysterious events)   **10**
relinquished . . . artists abandoned by the learned physicians   11 *both . . .
Paracelsus* of both schools of medical opinion   12 *authentic fellows* accred-
ited physicians   21 *in showing* visibly, in print   23–24 *A . . . actor* (Lafew
evidently reads from a printed ballad celebrating the king's recovery)   26
dolphin (a proverbially sportive creature; with pun on "dauphin," heir to the
throne of France, hence a playful princeling); *'Fore me* i.e., upon my soul (see
II.4.29–30)   27 *speak in respect* i.e., with no offense to the true dauphin   29
tedious long   29–30 *facinerious* wicked

LAFEW   Very hand of heaven –

PAROLLES   Ay, so I say.

LAFEW   In a most weak –

PAROLLES   And debile minister; great power, great tran-   34
scendence, which should indeed give us a further use to
be made than alone the recovery of the king, as to be –

LAFEW   Generally thankful.

    Enter King, Helena, and Attendants.

PAROLLES   I would have said it! you say well. Here comes
the king.

LAFEW   Lustick! as the Dutchman says. I'll like a maid   40
the better whilst I have a tooth in my head. Why, he's   41
able to lead her a coranto.   42

PAROLLES   *Mort du vinaigre!* Is not this Helen?   43

LAFEW   'Fore God, I think so.

KING

Go, call before me all the lords in court.

                             [Exit an Attendant.]

Sit, my preserver, by thy patient's side,

And with this healthful hand whose banished sense   47

Thou hast repealed, a second time receive   48

The confirmation of my promised gift,

Which but attends thy naming.   50

    Enter three or four Lords.

Fair maid, send forth thine eye. This youthful parcel   51

Of noble bachelors stand at my bestowing,   52

O'er whom both sovereign power and father's voice

I have to use. Thy frank election make.   54

Thou hast power to choose, and they none to forsake.

HELENA

To each of you one fair and virtuous mistress

---

34 *debile* feeble; *minister* agent (i.e., Helena)   40 *Lustick* lusty   41
whilst . . . head i.e., while still young   42 *coranto* lively dance   43 *Mort du
vinaigre* (expletive of obscure meaning; literally, "death by vinegar")   47
banished sense loss of sensation   48 *repealed* called back   50 *attends* awaits
51 *parcel* group   52 *stand . . . bestowing* are in my charge to bestow in marriage (i.e., the lords are the king's wards, as Helena is a ward of the countess:
see I.1.5 and I.1. 37–38)   54 *frank election* unhindered choice

Fall, when Love please; marry, to each but one.

LAFEW   *[Aside]*

58   I'd give bay curtal and his furniture

59   My mouth no more were broken than these boys',

60   And writ as little beard.

KING   Peruse them well:

Not one of those but had a noble father.

HELENA

Gentlemen,

Heaven hath through me restored the king to health.

ALL

We understand it, and thank heaven for you.

HELENA

I am a simple maid, and therein wealthiest

66   That I protest I simply am a maid.

Please it your majesty, I have done already.

The blushes in my cheeks thus whisper me,

69   "We blush that thou shouldst choose; but be refused,

70   Let the white death sit on thy cheek forever,

We'll ne'er come there again."

KING   Make choice and see;

Who shuns thy love shuns all his love in me.

HELENA

73   Now, Dian, from thy altar do I fly,

74   And to imperial Love, that god most high,

Do my sighs stream.

          She addresses her[self] to a Lord.

                              Sir, will you hear my suit?

FIRST LORD

76   And grant it.

HELENA   Thanks, sir, all the rest is mute.

---

58 *bay curtal* bay horse with docked tail; *furniture* trappings   **59** *My . . . boys'*
i.e., (1) if I still had all my teeth, (2) if I, like a young horse, were still unused
to the bit   **60** *writ* claimed; *Peruse* survey   **66** *simply* truly   **69** *be refused* if
you be refused   **70** *white* pale   **73** *Dian* Diana, goddess of chastity and the
hunt   **74** *Love* i.e., Cupid   **76** *all . . . mute* I have nothing more to say

LAFEW   *[Aside]* I had rather be in this choice than throw
amesace for my life.   78

HELENA   *[To another]*
The honor, sir, that flames in your fair eyes,
Before I speak, too threat'ningly replies.   80
Love make your fortunes twenty times above
Her that so wishes, and her humble love!   82

SECOND LORD
No better, if you please.   83

HELENA   My wish receive,
Which great Love grant; and so I take my leave.

LAFEW   *[Aside]* Do all they deny her? An they were sons   85
of mine, I'd have them whipped, or I would send them
to th' Turk to make eunuchs of.

HELENA   *[To a third]*
Be not afraid that I your hand should take;
I'll never do you wrong for your own sake.
Blessing upon your vows, and in your bed   90
Find fairer fortune, if you ever wed.

LAFEW   *[Aside]* These boys are boys of ice; they'll none
have her. Sure they are bastards to the English; the   93
French ne'er got 'em.

HELENA   *[To a fourth]*
You are too young, too happy, and too good,
To make yourself a son out of my blood.

FOURTH LORD
Fair one, I think not so.

LAFEW   *[Aside]* There's one grape yet; I am sure thy fa-   98
ther drunk wine. But if thou be'st not an ass, I am a
youth of fourteen; I have known thee already.   100

---

78 *amesace* a pair of aces, the lowest throw of the dice (Lafew is being ironic;
throughout the choosing scene, Lafew misinterprets what he sees and we
hear) 82 *Her* i.e., Helena 83 *No better* i.e., no better fortune than to be
chosen by you; *My wish receive* i.e., my wish, but not my love 85 *An* if 93
Sure certainly 98 *one grape* one scion of good stock 98–99 *thy . . . wine*
i.e., (1) good blood flows in your veins, (2) your father was red-blooded
100 *known* seen through

HELENA   *[To Bertram]*
    I dare not say I take you, but I give
    Me and my service, ever whilst I live,
    Into your guiding power. – This is the man.

KING
    Why then, young Bertram, take her; she's thy wife.

BERTRAM
    My wife, my liege? I shall beseech your highness,
    In such a business give me leave to use
    The help of mine own eyes.

KING   Know'st thou not, Bertram,
    What she has done for me?

BERTRAM   Yes, my good lord;
    But never hope to know why I should marry her.

KING
110   Thou know'st she has raised me from my sickly bed.

BERTRAM
111   But follows it, my lord, to bring me down
    Must answer for your raising? I know her well;
113   She had her breeding at my father's charge.
    A poor physician's daughter my wife? Disdain
115   Rather corrupt me ever!

KING
116   'Tis only title thou disdain'st in her, the which
117   I can build up. Strange is it that our bloods,
118   Of color, weight, and heat, poured all together,
119   Would quite confound distinction, yet stands off
120   In differences so mighty. If she be
    All that is virtuous – save what thou dislik'st,
    A poor physician's daughter – thou dislik'st
    Of virtue for the name. But do not so.
    From lowest place when virtuous things proceed,

---

111 *down* i.e., to a socially inferior match   113 *breeding* upbringing   115 *corrupt me ever* spoil my credit with you for as long as I live   116 *title* i.e., lack of a title   117 *build up* establish   118 *Of* in respect to   119 *confound distinction* merge indistinguishably   119–20 *stands . . . mighty* hold aloof as though totally different

The place is dignified by th' doer's deed.
Where great additions swell's, and virtue none,   126
It is a dropsied honor. Good alone   127
Is good without a name; vileness is so:
The property by what it is should go,   129
Not by the title. She is young, wise, fair;   *130*
In these to nature she's immediate heir;   131
And these breed honor. That is honor's scorn
Which challenges itself as honor's born   133
And is not like the sire. Honors thrive
When rather from our acts we them derive   135
Than our foregoers. The mere word's a slave,   136
Deboshed on every tomb, on every grave   137
A lying trophy, and as oft is dumb,   138
Where dust and damned oblivion is the tomb
Of honored bones indeed. What should be said?   140
If thou canst like this creature as a maid,
I can create the rest. Virtue and she
Is her own dower; honor and wealth from me.

BERTRAM
I cannot love her, nor will strive to do't.

KING
Thou wrong'st thyself if thou shouldst strive to choose.   145

HELENA
That you are well restored, my lord, I'm glad.
Let the rest go.

KING
My honor's at the stake, which to defeat,   148
I must produce my power. Here, take her hand,

---

126 *great additions swell's* solemn titles puff us up   127 *dropsied* unhealthily
swollen   129 *property* quality; *go* circulate (i.e., be publicly recognized)
131 *immediate* direct   133–34 *challenges . . . sire* claims descent from honorable stock but does not resemble it   135 *derive* inherit   136 *foregoers* fore-
bears   137 *Deboshed* debauched, debased   138 *lying* (1) deceitful, (2)
recumbent; *dumb* silent   140 *honored bones indeed* truly honorable bones
145 *strive to choose* attempt to choose for yourself   148 *at the stake* (like a
bear being baited); *which* which challenge

150   Proud scornful boy, unworthy this good gift,
151   That dost in vile misprision shackle up
       My love and her desert; that canst not dream,
153   We, poising us in her defective scale,
       Shall weigh thee to the beam; that wilt not know,
       It is in us to plant thine honor where
       We please to have it grow. Check thy contempt.
157   Obey our will, which travails in thy good.
158   Believe not thy disdain, but presently
159   Do thine own fortunes that obedient right
160   Which both thy duty owes and our power claims;
       Or I will throw thee from my care forever,
162   Into the staggers and the careless lapse
       Of youth and ignorance, both my revenge and hate
       Loosing upon thee, in the name of justice,
165   Without all terms of pity. Speak, thine answer.

BERTRAM
166   Pardon, my gracious lord; for I submit
167   My fancy to your eyes. When I consider
168   What great creation and what dole of honor
169   Flies where you bid it, I find that she, which late
170   Was in my nobler thoughts most base, is now
       The praisèd of the king; who, so ennobled,
       Is as 'twere born so.

KING   Take her by the hand,
       And tell her she is thine; to whom I promise
174   A counterpoise, if not to thy estate,
       A balance more replete.

BERTRAM   I take her hand.

----

151 *misprision* contempt (with pun on "false imprisonment"); *shackle up* i.e.,
paralyze, render useless   153–54 *poising . . . beam* weighing our royal self on
her side of the balance will outweigh your side and make it touch the cross-
bar   157 *travails* labors   158 *Believe not* do not trust to; *presently* instantly
159 *obedient right* right of obedience   162 *lapse* fall   165 *Without . . . pity*
without pity in any form   166 *submit* subdue   167 *fancy* affection, desire
168 *great creation* creation of greatness; *dole* share   169 *late* lately, earlier
174–75 *A counterpoise . . . replete* a counterweight, and even greater weight
(of wealth, by way of dowry), if not of nobility

KING
   Good fortune and the favor of the king
   Smile upon this contract, whose ceremony   177
   Shall seem expedient on the now-born brief,
   And be performed tonight. The solemn feast
   Shall more attend upon the coming space,   180
   Expecting absent friends. As thou lov'st her,   181
   Thy love's to me religious; else, does err.   182

Exeunt. Parolles and Lafew stay behind,
commenting of this wedding.

LAFEW   Do you hear, monsieur? A word with you.

PAROLLES   Your pleasure, sir?

LAFEW   Your lord and master did well to make his recantation.

PAROLLES   Recantation? my lord? my master?

LAFEW   Ay. Is it not a language I speak?

PAROLLES   A most harsh one, and not to be understood
without bloody succeeding. My master?   190

LAFEW   Are you companion to the Count Rossillion?   191

PAROLLES   To any count; to all counts; to what is man.   192

LAFEW   To what is count's man; count's master is of another style.   193

PAROLLES   You are too old, sir. Let it satisfy you, you are   195
too old.

LAFEW   I must tell thee, sirrah, I write man, to which   197
title age cannot bring thee.

PAROLLES   What I dare too well do, I dare not do.   199

LAFEW   I did think thee, for two ordinaries, to be a pretty   200
wise fellow; thou didst make tolerable vent of thy   201

177–78 *whose . . . brief* the consecration of which fittingly follows without
delay in this fresh agreement   180 *more . . . space* be deferred a while longer
181 *Expecting* while we await   182 *religious* scrupulous   190 *bloody succeeding* bloodshed following   191 *companion* fellow (used belittlingly)   192
what is man any true man   193 *count's man* servant   195 *too old* i.e., for me
to thrash   197 *write man* claim manhood   199 *What . . . not do* what I can
do all too easily – beat you – the privilege of your age forbids me to do   200
ordinaries meals   201 *make tolerable vent of* discourse tolerably upon

202   travel; it might pass. Yet the scarfs and the bannerets
       about thee did manifoldly dissuade me from believing
204   thee a vessel of too great a burden. I have now found
       thee; when I lose thee again, I care not. Yet art thou
206   good for nothing but taking up, and that thou'rt scarce
       worth.

PAROLLES   Hadst thou not the privilege of antiquity
       upon thee –

210 LAFEW   Do not plunge thyself too far in anger, lest thou
       hasten thy trial; which if – Lord have mercy on thee for
212   a hen! So, my good window of lattice, fare thee well;
213   thy casement I need not open, for I look through thee.
       Give me thy hand.

PAROLLES   My lord, you give me most egregious indig-
       nity.

LAFEW   Ay, with all my heart; and thou art worthy of it.

PAROLLES   I have not, my lord, deserved it.

219 LAFEW   Yes, good faith, every dram of it, and I will not
220   bate thee a scruple.

PAROLLES   Well, I shall be wiser.

222 LAFEW   Ev'n as soon as thou canst, for thou hast to pull
       at a smack o' th' contrary. If ever thou be'st bound in
       thy scarf and beaten, thou shall find what it is to be
225   proud of thy bondage. I have a desire to hold my ac-
       quaintance with thee, or rather my knowledge, that I
227   may say, in the default, "He is a man I know."

PAROLLES   My lord, you do me most insupportable vexa-
       tion.

---

202 *scarfs* sashes (commonly worn over the shoulder or around the waist by
soldiers); *bannerets* scarves, looking like a ship's pennants   204 *burden* cargo;
found seen through   206 *taking up* purchasing at a discount, as surplus mer-
chandise   212 *hen* i.e., a female of your kind; *lattice* (the red-latticed window was the mark of an alehouse)   213 *casement* window; *look* see   219
dram bit, eighth of an ounce   220 *bate* deduct; *scruple* third of a dram
222–23 *pull . . . contrary* take a swig from the large amount of foolishness in
yourself   225 *your bondage* what binds (i.e., the *scarf*)   227 *in the default*
when you are weighed and found wanting

LAFEW   I would it were hell pains for thy sake, and my   *230*
poor doing eternal; for doing I am past, as I will by   *231*
thee, in what motion age will give me leave.   *Exit.*   *232*

PAROLLES   Well, thou hast a son shall take this disgrace
off me, scurvy, old, filthy, scurvy lord! Well, I must be
patient; there is no fettering of authority. I'll beat him,
by my life, if I can meet him with any convenience, an   *236*
he were double and double a lord. I'll have no more
pity of his age than I would have of – I'll beat him, an
if I could but meet him again.

   Enter Lafew.

LAFEW   Sirrah, your lord and master's married; there's   *240*
news for you. You have a new mistress.

PAROLLES   I most unfeignedly beseech your lordship to
make some reservation of your wrongs. He is my good   *243*
lord; whom I serve above is my master.

LAFEW   Who? God?

PAROLLES   Ay, sir.

LAFEW   The devil it is that's thy master. Why dost thou
garter up thy arms o' this fashion? Dost make hose of   *248*
thy sleeves? Do other servants so? Thou wert best set
thy lower part where thy nose stands. By mine honor, if   *250*
I were but two hours younger, I'd beat thee. Methink'st
thou art a general offense, and every man should beat   *252*
thee. I think thou wast created for men to breathe   *253*
themselves upon thee.

PAROLLES   This is hard and undeserved measure, my
lord.

LAFEW   Go to, sir. You were beaten in Italy for picking a   *257*
kernel out of a pomegranate. You are a vagabond, and
no true traveler. You are more saucy with lords and

---

231 *doing* activity of any kind, especially sexual   **231–32** *by thee* i.e., pass by
thee   **232** *in what motion* with what speed   **236** *an* if   **243** *make . . .
wrongs* place some limit to your insults   **248** *garter up* i.e., bind decorative
scarves around your sleeves (usually reserved for stockings); *hose* stockings
252 *general offense* public nuisance   **253** *breathe* exercise   **257–58** *picking . . . pomegranate* i.e., some petty misdemeanor (?)

260 honorable personages than the commission of your
261 birth and virtue gives you heraldry. You are not worth
another word, else I'd call you knave. I leave you. *Exit.*
Enter [Bertram] Count Rossillion.

PAROLLES   Good, very good! It is so then. Good, very
264 good! Let it be concealed awhile.

BERTRAM
Undone, and forfeited to cares forever!

PAROLLES
What's the matter, sweetheart?

BERTRAM
Although before the solemn priest I have sworn,
I will not bed her.

PAROLLES
What? what, sweetheart?

BERTRAM
270 O my Parolles, they have married me!
I'll to the Tuscan wars and never bed her.

PAROLLES
272 France is a doghole, and it no more merits
The tread of a man's foot. To th' wars!

BERTRAM
There's letters from my mother. What th' import is,
I know not yet.

PAROLLES
Ay, that would be known. To th' wars, my boy, to th'
wars!
277 He wears his honor in a box unseen
278 That hugs his kicky-wicky here at home,
279 Spending his manly marrow in her arms,
280 Which should sustain the bound and high curvet
Of Mars's fiery steed. To other regions!
282 France is a stable; we that dwell in't jades.

---

261 *heraldry* authority, warrant 264 *it* i.e., the truth of Parolles' character
272 *doghole* i.e., unfit for human habitation 277 *box* (with sexual suggestion of female genitalia) 278 *kicky-wicky* (contemptuous term for woman)
279 *Spending . . . marrow* draining his manhood (through sexual ejacula-
tion) 280 *curvet* leap 282 *jades* nags, inferior horses

Therefore to th' war!

BERTRAM

It shall be so. I'll send her to my house,
Acquaint my mother with my hate to her,
And wherefore I am fled; write to the king
That which I durst not speak. His present gift
Shall furnish me to those Italian fields   288
Where noble fellows strike. Wars is no strife   289
To the dark house and the detested wife.   290

PAROLLES

Will this capriccio hold in thee, art sure?   291

BERTRAM

Go with me to my chamber and advise me.
I'll send her straight away. Tomorrow
I'll to the wars, she to her single sorrow.

PAROLLES

Why, these balls bound; there's noise in it! 'Tis hard: 295
A young man married is a man that's marred.
Therefore away, and leave her bravely; go.   297
The king has done you wrong; but hush, 'tis so.

                                     Exeunt.

*

∾ **II.4** *Enter Helena and [Lavatch, the] Clown.*

HELENA

My mother greets me kindly. Is she well?

LAVATCH   She is not well, but yet she has her health; she's   2
very merry, but yet she is not well. But thanks be given,
she's very well and wants nothing i' th' world. But yet
she is not well.

HELENA   If she be very well, what does she ail that she's
not very well?

---

288 *furnish* equip **289** *no strife / To* no competition in comparison with
290 *dark house* madhouse **291** *capriccio* whim **295** *balls* tennis balls;
bound bounce; *there's . . . it* i.e., you really mean it **297** *bravely* boldly

    II.4 The palace of the king **2** *not well* (evidently alluding to the prover-
bial belief that all is well with the dead; see l. 11)

LAVATCH   Truly she's very well indeed, but for two things.

10   HELENA   What two things?

LAVATCH   One, that she's not in heaven, whither God send her quickly; the other, that she's in earth, from whence God send her quickly.

Enter Parolles.

PAROLLES   Bless you, my fortunate lady!

HELENA   I hope, sir, I have your good will to have mine own good fortune.

PAROLLES   You had my prayers to lead them on, and to keep them on have them still. O, my knave, how does my old lady?

20   LAVATCH   So that you had her wrinkles and I her money,
21   I would she did as you say.

PAROLLES   Why, I say nothing.

LAVATCH   Marry, you are the wiser man; for many a man's tongue shakes out his master's undoing. To say nothing, to do nothing, to know nothing, and to have
26   nothing, is to be a great part of your title, which is within a very little of nothing.

PAROLLES   Away! th' art a knave.

29   LAVATCH   You should have said, sir, "Before a knave th'
30   art a knave"; that's "Before me th' art a knave." This had been truth, sir.

32   PAROLLES   Go to, thou art a witty fool; I have found thee.

34   LAVATCH   Did you find me in yourself, sir, or were you taught to find me? [. . .] The search, sir, was profitable;
36   and much fool may you find in you, even to the world's pleasure and the increase of laughter.

38   PAROLLES   A good knave, i' faith, and well fed.

Madam, my lord will go away tonight;

---

21 *I . . . say* (meaning obscure)   26 *be . . . title* be very like you, in status and possessions   29 *Before* in presence of   30 *Before me* "upon my word" (with pun on "ahead of me")   32–33 *found thee* found thee out   34 *in yourself* unaided   36 *much . . . in you* much folly may you find in yourself   38 *well fed* i.e., well fed and ill taught (see II.2.3)

A very serious business calls on him.   40
The great prerogative and rite of love,   41
Which, as your due, time claims, he does acknowledge;   42
But puts it off to a compelled restraint;   43
Whose want, and whose delay, is strewed with sweets,   44
Which they distill now in the curbèd time,   45
To make the coming hour o'erflow with joy
And pleasure drown the brim.   47

HELENA   What's his will else?

PAROLLES
That you will take your instant leave o' th' king,
And make this haste as your own good proceeding,   49
Strengthened with what apology you think   50
May make it probable need.   51

HELENA   What more commands he?

PAROLLES
That, having this obtained, you presently   52
Attend his further pleasure.   53

HELENA
In everything I wait upon his will.   54

PAROLLES
I shall report it so.   *Exit Parolles.*

HELENA
I pray you. Come, sirrah.   *Exit [with Lavatch].*

                              *

∾ **II.5** *Enter Lafew and Bertram.*

LAFEW   But I hope your lordship thinks not him a soldier.

---

41 *rite of love* i.e., sexual consummation of the marriage   42 *time* i.e., present time   43 *to* in consequence of   44 *Whose* (referring to the *rite of love*);
want lack; *sweets* i.e., the delay sweetens the eventual accomplishment of the
rite of love as flowers perfume a marriage bed   45 *they* i.e., *want* and *delay*;
curbèd time period of distillation   47 *else* besides   49 *make* represent; *proceeding* plan   51 *probable* plausible   52 *presently* immediately   53 *Attend*
await   54 *wait upon* serve
  II.5 The palace of the king

3   BERTRAM   Yes, my lord, and of very valiant approof.

     LAFEW   You have it from his own deliverance.

     BERTRAM   And by other warranted testimony.

6   LAFEW   Then my dial goes not true; I took this lark for a
7   bunting.

     BERTRAM   I do assure you, my lord, he is very great in
9   knowledge and accordingly valiant.

10   LAFEW   I have then sinned against his experience and
11   transgressed against his valor; and my state that way is
     dangerous, since I cannot yet find in my heart to re-
     pent.

          Enter Parolles.

     Here he comes. I pray you make us friends; I will pur-
     sue the amity.

     PAROLLES   *[To Bertram]* These things shall be done, sir.

17   LAFEW   Pray you, sir, who's his tailor?

     PAROLLES   Sir?

     LAFEW   O, I know him well, I, sir. He, sir, 's a good
20   workman, a very good tailor.

     BERTRAM   *[Aside to Parolles]*
     Is she gone to the king?

     PAROLLES   She is.

     BERTRAM
     Will she away tonight?

     PAROLLES   As you'll have her.

     BERTRAM
     I have writ my letters, casketed my treasure,
     Given order for our horses; and tonight,
     When I should take possession of the bride,
     End ere I do begin.

27   LAFEW   A good traveler is something at the latter end of a
28   dinner; but one that lies three thirds and uses a known

---

3 *very valiant approof* proved valor   **6** *my dial* the compass of my judgment
7 *bunting* common field bird   **9** *accordingly* correspondingly   **11–12** *my . . .
dangerous* my soul is in peril   **17** *who's his tailor* i.e., who made this man-
nequin   **27–28** *at . . . dinner* i.e., to relate his travels   **28** *three thirds* i.e., all
the time

truth to pass a thousand nothings with, should be once
heard and thrice beaten. God save you, captain.   30

BERTRAM   Is there any unkindness between my lord and   31
you, monsieur?

PAROLLES   I know not how I have deserved to run into
my lord's displeasure.

LAFEW   You have made shift to run into't, boots and   35
spurs and all, like him that leapt into the custard; and   36
out of it you'll run again rather than suffer question for   37
your residence.

BERTRAM   It may be you have mistaken him, my lord.   39

LAFEW   And shall do so ever, though I took him at's   40
prayers. Fare you well, my lord, and believe this of me:
there can be no kernel in this light nut; the soul of this
man is his clothes. Trust him not in matter of heavy   43
consequence. I have kept of them tame and know their   44
natures. – Farewell, monsieur. I have spoken better of
you than you have or will to deserve at my hand; but
we must do good against evil.   *[Exit.]*   47

PAROLLES   An idle lord, I swear.   48

BERTRAM   I think so.   49

PAROLLES   Why, do you not know him?   50

BERTRAM
Yes, I do know him well, and common speech
Gives him a worthy pass.   52
      Enter Helena.
                              Here comes my clog.

HELENA
I have, sir, as I was commanded from you,

---

31 *unkindness* ill feeling 35 *made shift* contrived 36 *him . . . custard* the
clown who jumped into the custard at the yearly Lord Mayor's feast 37–38
suffer . . . residence explain your presence there (i.e., consider why you have
displeased me) 39 *mistaken* misjudged 40 *do so* mistake, put an unfavor-
able interpretation on 43 *heavy* serious 44 *kept . . . tame* kept such creatures household pets 47 *we . . . evil* (see I Thessalonians 5:15) 48 *an idle* a
foolish 49 *I . . . so* (This line is frequently emended to read "I think not so";
the same doubt can be conveyed through use of tone.) 52 *pass* reputation;
clog hobble (a fetter designed to hinder a horse's movement)

Spoke with the king, and have procured his leave
55 For present parting; only he desires
Some private speech with you.
BERTRAM   I shall obey his will.
You must not marvel, Helen, at my course,
58 Which holds not color with the time, nor does
The ministration and required office
60 On my particular. Prepared I was not
For such a business; therefore am I found
So much unsettled. This drives me to entreat you
That presently you take your way for home,
64 And rather muse than ask why I entreat you;
65 For my respects are better than they seem,
66 And my appointments have in them a need
Greater than shows itself at the first view
To you that know them not. This to my mother.
    [Gives a letter.]
'Twill be two days ere I shall see you; so
70 I leave you to your wisdom.
HELENA   Sir, I can nothing say
But that I am your most obedient servant.
BERTRAM
Come, come; no more of that.
HELENA   And ever shall
73 With true observance seek to eke out that
74 Wherein toward me my homely stars have failed
To equal my great fortune.
BERTRAM   Let that go;
My haste is very great. Farewell. Hie home.
HELENA
Pray, sir, your pardon.
BERTRAM   Well, what would you say?

---

55 *present* immediate   58 *holds . . . time* seems inappropriate to the occasion
58–60 *nor . . . particular* nor fulfills my obligations as a husband   64 *muse*
remain in wonder   65 *respects* reasons   66 *appointments* arrangements   73
observance dutiful service; *eke out* supplement   74 *homely stars* humble ori-
gins

HELENA

   I am not worthy of the wealth I owe,   78
   Nor dare I say 'tis mine; and yet it is –
   But, like a timorous thief, most fain would steal   80
   What law does vouch mine own.   81

BERTRAM   What would you have?

HELENA

   Something, and scarce so much; nothing, indeed.
   I would not tell you what I would, my lord.
   Faith, yes –
   Strangers and foes do sunder, and not kiss.   85

BERTRAM

   I pray you stay not, but in haste to horse.

HELENA

   I shall not break your bidding, good my lord.

BERTRAM

   Where are my other men, monsieur? Farewell.
   Go thou toward home –   *Exit [Helena].*
               where I will never come
   Whilst I can shake my sword or hear the drum.   90
   Away, and for our flight!   91

PAROLLES   Bravely, *coraggio!*   *[Exeunt.]*

               *

∾ **III.1** *Flourish. Enter the Duke of Florence, the two*
    Frenchmen, with a troop of Soldiers.

DUKE

   So that from point to point now have you heard
   The fundamental reasons of this war,
   Whose great decision hath much blood let forth,   3
   And more thirsts after.

---

78 *owe* own   80 *fain* gladly   81 *vouch* confirm   85 *sunder* part   91 *coraggio*
courage

   III.1 The palace of the Duke of Florence   3 *Whose great decision* the de-
ciding of which

FIRST LORD   Holy seems the quarrel
   Upon your grace's part; black and fearful
   On the opposer.

DUKE
7   Therefore we marvel much our cousin France
   Would in so just a business shut his bosom
9   Against our borrowing prayers.

SECOND LORD   Good my lord,
10   The reasons of our state I cannot yield
11   But like a common and an outward man
   That the great figure of a council frames
   By self-unable motion – therefore dare not
   Say what I think of it, since I have found
   Myself in my incertain grounds to fail
   As often as I guessed.

DUKE   Be it his pleasure.

FIRST LORD
17   But I am sure the younger of our nature,
18   That surfeit on their ease, will day by day
19   Come here for physic.

DUKE   Welcome shall they be;
20   And all the honors that can fly from us
   Shall on them settle. You know your places well;
22   When better fall, for your avails they fell.
   Tomorrow to th' field.   *Flourish. [Exeunt.]*

*

 ❧ **III.2** *Enter Countess and [Lavatch, the] Clown.*

COUNTESS   It hath happened all as I would have had it,
save that he comes not along with her.

---

7 *cousin* fellow ruler   9 *borrowing prayers* prayers for aid   10 *yield* report
11–13 *a common . . . motion* an unskilled outsider who imperfectly imagines
to himself the great deliberations proceeding in secret   17 *nature* disposition
18 *surfeit on their ease* grow sick of leisure   19 *physic* medicine   22
When . . . fell when better places fall vacant, they will become yours
   III.2 The palace of the Countess of Rossillion

LAVATCH   By my troth, I take my young lord to be a very
melancholy man.

COUNTESS   By what observance, I pray you?   5

LAVATCH   Why, he will look upon his boot, and sing;
mend the ruff, and sing; ask questions, and sing; pick   7
his teeth, and sing. I know a man that had this trick of   8
melancholy sold a goodly manor for a song.

COUNTESS   Let me see what he writes, and when he   10
means to come.
        [Opens a letter.]

LAVATCH   I have no mind to Isbel since I was at court.
Our old lings and our Isbels o' th' country are nothing   13
like your old ling and your Isbels o' th' court. The
brains of my Cupid's knocked out, and I begin to love,
as an old man loves money, with no stomach.   16

COUNTESS   What have we here?

LAVATCH   E'en that you have there.   *Exit.*

[COUNTESS] *[Reads] a letter.* "I have sent you a daughter-
in-law. She hath recovered the king and undone me. I   20
have wedded her, not bedded her, and sworn to make
the 'not' eternal. You shall hear I am run away; know it   22
before the report come. If there be breadth enough in
the world, I will hold a long distance. My duty to you.
                            Your unfortunate son,
                                            Bertram."

This is not well, rash and unbridled boy,
To fly the favors of so good a king,
To pluck his indignation on thy head
By the misprizing of a maid too virtuous   30
For the contempt of empire.   31
        Enter [Lavatch, the] Clown.

---

5 *observance* observation   7 *mend the ruff* adjust his boot cuff   8 *trick* cus-
tom, habit   13 *old lings* salted cods (slang for penis)   16 *stomach* appetite,
inclination   20 *recovered* cured   22 *not* (with pun on virgin "knot" – i.e.,
hymen)   30 *misprizing* scorning   31 *For . . . empire* for even an emperor to
scorn

LAVATCH   O madam, yonder is heavy news within between two soldiers and my young lady!

COUNTESS   What is the matter?

LAVATCH   Nay, there is some comfort in the news, some
36   comfort – your son will not be killed so soon as I
thought he would.

COUNTESS   Why should he be killed?

LAVATCH   So say I, madam, if he run away, as I hear he
40   does. The danger is in standing to't; that's the loss of
41   men, though it be the getting of children. Here they
come will tell you more. For my part, I only hear your
son was run away.   *[Exit.]*
   Enter Helena and [the] two [French] Gentlemen.

SECOND LORD   Save you, good madam.

HELENA
   Madam, my lord is gone, forever gone!

FIRST LORD   Do not say so.

COUNTESS
   Think upon patience. Pray you, gentlemen –
48   I have felt so many quirks of joy and grief
49   That the first face of neither on the start
50   Can woman me unto't. Where is my son, I pray you?

FIRST LORD
   Madam, he's gone to serve the Duke of Florence.
   We met him thitherward, for thence we came;
53   And after some dispatch in hand at court,
   Thither we bend again.

55   HELENA   Look on his letter, madam. Here's my passport.
   [Reads.] "When thou canst get the ring upon my finger,
   which never shall come off, and show me a child begotten of thy body that I am father to, then call me husband; but in such a 'then' I write a 'never.'"
60   This is a dreadful sentence.

----

36 *be killed* "die" sexually, in orgasm   40 *standing to't* meeting danger head
on (with sexual meaning of becoming erect)   41 *getting* begetting   48
quirks spells   49 *face* appearance; *on the start* suddenly   50 *woman me* make
me womanish (i.e., weep)   53 *dispatch* business   55 *passport* beggar's license

COUNTESS
   Brought you this letter, gentlemen?
FIRST LORD   Ay, madam,
   And for the contents' sake are sorry for our pains.
COUNTESS
   I prithee, lady, have a better cheer.
   If thou engrossest all the griefs are thine,   64
   Thou robb'st me of a moiety. He was my son,   65
   But I do wash his name out of my blood,
   And thou art all my child. Towards Florence is he?   67
FIRST LORD
   Ay, madam.
COUNTESS   And to be a soldier?
FIRST LORD
   Such is his noble purpose, and believe't,
   The duke will lay upon him all the honor   70
   That good convenience claims.   71
COUNTESS   Return you thither?
SECOND LORD
   Ay, madam, with the swiftest wing of speed.
HELENA   *[Reads.]*
   "Till I have no wife, I have nothing in France."
   'Tis bitter.
COUNTESS   Find you that there?
HELENA   Ay, madam.
SECOND LORD   'Tis but the boldness of his hand haply,   75
   which his heart was not consenting to.
COUNTESS
   Nothing in France until he have no wife!
   There's nothing here that is too good for him
   But only she, and she deserves a lord
   That twenty such rude boys might tend upon   80
   And call her hourly mistress. Who was with him?
SECOND LORD
   A servant only, and a gentleman

---

64 *engrossest* monopolize; *are* that are   65 *moiety* half   67 *all my child* my
only child   71 *convenience* fitness   75 *haply* perhaps

Which I have sometime known.

COUNTESS   Parolles, was it not?

SECOND LORD
Ay, my good lady, he.

COUNTESS
85   A very tainted fellow, and full of wickedness.
86   My son corrupts a well-derivèd nature
87   With his inducement.

SECOND LORD   Indeed, good lady,
88   The fellow has a deal of that too much
Which holds him much to have.

COUNTESS   You're welcome, gentlemen.
90   I will entreat you, when you see my son,
To tell him that his sword can never win
The honor that he loses. More I'll entreat you
93   Written to bear along.

FIRST LORD   We serve you, madam,
In that and all your worthiest affairs.

COUNTESS
95   Not so, but as we change our courtesies.
96   Will you draw near?   *Exit [with the Gentlemen].*

HELENA
"Till I have no wife I have nothing in France."
Nothing in France until he has no wife!
Thou shalt have none, Rossillion, none in France;
100   Then hast thou all again. Poor lord, is't I
That chase thee from thy country, and expose
102   Those tender limbs of thine to the event
Of the none-sparing war? And is it I
That drive thee from the sportive court, where thou
105   Wast shot at with fair eyes, to be the mark

---

85 *tainted* depraved   86 *a well-derivèd nature* inherited goodness   87 *With his inducement* by his (Parolles') ill counsel   88–89 *has . . . have* possesses just the sort of superfluity that endears him to Bertram   93 *Written* in writing   95 *Not so . . . courtesies* you serve me only in the sense that we mutually serve each other   96 *draw near* come in   102 *event* outcome   105 *mark* target

Of smoky muskets? O you leaden messengers
That ride upon the violent speed of fire,
Fly with false aim; move the still-piecing air,   108
That sings with piercing; do not touch my lord!
Whoever shoots at him, I set him there.   110
Whoever charges on his forward breast,
I am the caitiff that do hold him to't.   112
And though I kill him not, I am the cause
His death was so effected. Better 'twere
I met the ravin lion when he roared   115
With sharp constraint of hunger; better 'twere
That all the miseries which nature owes   117
Were mine at once. No; come thou home, Rossillion,
Whence honor but of danger wins a scar,   119
As oft it loses all. I will be gone.   120
My being here it is that holds thee hence.
Shall I stay here to do't? No, no, although
The air of paradise did fan the house
And angels officed all. I will be gone,   124
That pitiful rumor may report my flight   125
To consolate thine ear. Come, night; end, day;   126
For with the dark, poor thief, I'll steal away.   *Exit.*

*

ᴥ **III.3** *Flourish. Enter the Duke of Florence,*
[Bertram Count] Rossillion, Drum and Trumpets,
Soldiers, Parolles.

DUKE

The general of our horse thou art; and we,   1
Great in our hope, lay our best love and credence   2

---

108 *still-piecing* always closing again   **112** *caitiff* wretch   **115** *ravin* raven-
ous   **117** *owes* owns   **119–20** *Whence . . . all* from where honor wins nothing from danger but scars, and sometimes pays with its life   **124** *officed all*
did all the household chores   **125** *pitiful* i.e., full of pity for Bertram   **126**
consolate console

III.3 The palace of the Duke of Florence   **1** *horse* cavalry troops   **2**
Great pregnant

    Upon thy promising fortune.

BERTRAM   Sir, it is
    A charge too heavy for my strength, but yet
    We'll strive to bear it for your worthy sake
6   To th' extreme edge of hazard.

DUKE   Then go thou forth,
    And Fortune play upon thy prosperous helm
    As thy auspicious mistress!

BERTRAM   This very day,
9   Great Mars, I put myself into thy file.
10   Make me but like my thoughts, and I shall prove
11   A lover of thy drum, hater of love.   *Exeunt omnes.*

                *

∾ **III.4** *Enter Countess and Steward.*

COUNTESS
    Alas! and would you take the letter of her?
    Might you not know she would do as she has done,
    By sending me a letter? Read it again.

[STEWARD] *[Reads the] letter.*
    "I am Saint Jaques' pilgrim, thither gone.
        Ambitious love hath so in me offended
    That barefoot plod I the cold ground upon,
        With sainted vow my faults to have amended.
    Write, write, that from the bloody course of war
9   My dearest master, your dear son, may hie.
10   Bless him at home in peace, whilst I from far
11   His name with zealous fervor sanctify.
12   His taken labors bid him me forgive.
13   I, his despiteful Juno, sent him forth
    From courtly friends, with camping foes to live,

---

6 *edge of hazard* limit of danger   9 *file* ranks   10 *like my thoughts* i.e., valiant
11 s.d. *omnes* all
    III.4 The palace of the Countess of Rossillion   9 *hie* hurry (to return)
11 *His . . . sanctify* (see I.1.100)   12 *taken* undertaken   13 *despiteful* spiteful; *Juno* goddess who assigned Hercules twelve labors

Where death and danger dogs the heels of worth.
He is too good and fair for death and me;
Whom I myself embrace to set him free."   17

COUNTESS
Ah, what sharp stings are in her mildest words!
Rinaldo, you did never lack advice so much   19
As letting her pass so. Had I spoke with her,   20
I could have well diverted her intents,
Which thus she hath prevented.   22

STEWARD   Pardon me, madam.
If I had given you this at overnight,   23
She might have been o'erta'en; and yet she writes
Pursuit would be but vain.

COUNTESS   What angel shall
Bless this unworthy husband? He cannot thrive,
Unless her prayers, whom heaven delights to hear
And loves to grant, reprieve him from the wrath
Of greatest justice. Write, write, Rinaldo,
To this unworthy husband of his wife.   30
Let every word weigh heavy of her worth
That he does weigh too light. My greatest grief,   32
Though little he do feel it, set down sharply.
Dispatch the most convenient messenger.
When haply he shall hear that she is gone,   35
He will return; and hope I may that she,
Hearing so much, will speed her foot again,
Led hither by pure love. Which of them both
Is dearest to me, I have no skill in sense   39
To make distinction. Provide this messenger.   40
My heart is heavy, and mine age is weak.
Grief would have tears, and sorrow bids me speak.
                                        Exeunt.

                    *

---

17 *Whom* death; *him* Bertram   19 *advice* judgment   22 *prevented* fore-
stalled   23 *at overnight* last night   32 *weigh* value   35 *haply* perchance   39
skill ability; *sense* feeling

❧ **III.5** *A tucket afar off. Enter old Widow of Florence,*
her Daughter [Diana], Violenta, and Mariana, with
other Citizens.

WIDOW Nay, come; for if they do approach the city, we
shall lose all the sight.

DIANA They say the French count has done most honorable service.

WIDOW It is reported that he has taken their great'st
commander, and that with his own hand he slew the
duke's brother. *[Tucket.]* We have lost our labor; they
are gone a contrary way. Hark! You may know by their
trumpets.

10 MARIANA Come, let's return again, and suffice ourselves
with the report of it. Well, Diana, take heed of this
12 French earl. The honor of a maid is her name, and no
13 legacy is so rich as honesty.

14 WIDOW I have told my neighbor how you have been solicited by a gentleman his companion.

MARIANA I know that knave, hang him! one Parolles, a
17 filthy officer he is in those suggestions for the young
earl. Beware of them, Diana; their promises, entice-
19 ments, oaths, tokens, and all these engines of lust, are
20 not the things they go under. Many a maid hath been
21 seduced by them; and the misery is, example, that so
terrible shows in the wrack of maidenhood, cannot for
23 all that dissuade succession but that they are limed with
the twigs that threatens them. I hope I need not to advise you further, but I hope your own grace will keep

---

III.5 The highway approaching Florence **s.d.** *tucket* trumpet fanfare **10** *suf-*
fice satisfy **12** *name* reputation for chastity **13** *honesty* chastity **14** *my*
neighbor i.e., Mariana **17** *officer* agent **19** *engines* artifices **20** *go under*
pretend to be **21** *example* precedent **21–22** *so . . . maidenhood* is so filled
with terrifying instances of virginity destroyed **23** *dissuade succession* dis-
courage others from following the same course; *they* i.e., other maidens
23–24 *limed . . . twigs* caught in snares (birdlime was applied to twigs to trap
birds)

you where you are, though there were no further dan-   26
ger known but the modesty which is so lost.

DIANA   You shall not need to fear me.   28

    Enter Helena [like a pilgrim].

WIDOW   I hope so. Look, here comes a pilgrim. I know
she will lie at my house; thither they send one another.   30
I'll question her. God save you, pilgrim! Whither are
you bound?

HELENA
To Saint Jaques le Grand.
Where do the palmers lodge, I do beseech you?   34

WIDOW
At the Saint Francis here, beside the port.   35

HELENA
Is this the way?

WIDOW
Ay, marry, is't.   37

    A march afar.

             Hark you! they come this way.
If you will tarry, holy pilgrim,
But till the troops come by,
I will conduct you where you shall be lodged,   40
The rather for I think I know your hostess
As ample as myself.   42

HELENA   Is it yourself?

WIDOW
If you shall please so, pilgrim.

HELENA
I thank you, and will stay upon your leisure.   44

WIDOW
You came, I think, from France?

HELENA   I did so.

26–27 *further danger* i.e., pregnancy   28 *fear* mistrust   30 *lie* lodge   34
palmers pilgrims   35 *the Saint Francis* (an inn); *port* city gate   37 *marry* indeed   42 *ample* well   44 *stay upon* await

WIDOW
   Here you shall see a countryman of yours
   That has done worthy service.
HELENA   His name, I pray you?
DIANA
   The Count Rossillion. Know you such a one?
HELENA
   But by the ear, that hears most nobly of him;
50   His face I know not.
DIANA   Whatsome'er he is,
51   He's bravely taken here. He stole from France,
   As 'tis reported, for the king had married him
   Against his liking. Think you it is so?
HELENA
54   Ay, surely, mere the truth; I know his lady.
DIANA
   There is a gentleman that serves the count
   Reports but coarsely of her.
HELENA   What's his name?
DIANA
   Monsieur Parolles.
HELENA   O, I believe with him,
58   In argument of praise or to the worth
59   Of the great count himself, she is too mean
60   To have her name repeated. All her deserving
61   Is a reservèd honesty, and that
62   I have not heard examined.
DIANA   Alas, poor lady!
   'Tis a hard bondage to become the wife
   Of a detesting lord.
WIDOW
65   I write, good creature, whereso'er she is,
   Her heart weighs sadly. This young maid might do her

---

51 *He's bravely taken* he has made a splendid impression   **54** *mere the truth* the
absolute truth   **58** *In argument of* as a subject of; *to* compared to   **59** *mean*
base   **60** *All her deserving* her only merit   **61** *reservèd honesty* preserved
chastity   **62** *examined* called into question   **65** *write* certify, declare

A shrewd turn, if she pleased.   67
HELENA   How do you mean?
May be the amorous count solicits her
In the unlawful purpose.
WIDOW   He does indeed,
And brokes with all that can in such a suit   70
Corrupt the tender honor of a maid;
But she is armed for him, and keeps her guard
In honestest defense.
      Drum and Colors. Enter [Bertram] Count Rossillion,
      Parolles, and the whole Army.
MARIANA   The gods forbid else!
WIDOW
So, now they come.
That is Antonio, the duke's eldest son;
That, Escalus.
HELENA   Which is the Frenchman?
DIANA   He –
That with the plume. 'Tis a most gallant fellow;
I would he loved his wife. If he were honester,   78
He were much goodlier. Is't not a handsome gentleman?
HELENA
I like him well.   80
DIANA
'Tis pity he is not honest. Yond's that same knave
That leads him to these places. Were I his lady,   82
I would poison that vile rascal.
HELENA   Which is he?
DIANA
That jackanapes with scarfs. Why is he melancholy?   84
HELENA
Perchance he's hurt i' th' battle.
PAROLLES   Lose our drum? Well!
MARIANA   He's shrewdly vexed at something. Look, he   87
has spied us.

---

67 *shrewd* mischievous   70 *brokes* bargains   78 *honester* more honorable
82 *places* infamous actions   84 *jackanapes* fool   87 *shrewdly* sorely

WIDOW   Marry, hang you!

90   MARIANA   And your curtsy, for a ring-carrier!

Exeunt [Bertram, Parolles, and Army].

WIDOW

The troop is past. Come, pilgrim, I will bring you

92   Where you shall host. Of enjoined penitents
There's four or five, to great Saint Jaques bound,
Already at my house.

HELENA   I humbly thank you.
Please it this matron and this gentle maid

96   To eat with us tonight, the charge and thanking
Shall be for me; and, to requite you further,

98   I will bestow some precepts of this virgin,
Worthy the note.

BOTH   We'll take your offer kindly.   *Exeunt.*

*

& **III.6** *Enter [Bertram] Count Rossillion and the
Frenchmen, as at first.*

1   SECOND LORD   Nay, good my lord, put him to't; let him
have his way.

3   FIRST LORD   If your lordship finds him not a hilding,
hold me no more in your respect.

5   SECOND LORD   On my life, my lord, a bubble.

BERTRAM   Do you think I am so far deceived in him?

SECOND LORD   Believe it, my lord, in mine own direct

8   knowledge, without any malice, but to speak of him as
my kinsman, he's a most notable coward, an infinite

10   and endless liar, an hourly promise-breaker, the owner

11   of no one good quality worthy your lordship's entertainment.

---

90 *curtsy* ceremony; *ring-carrier* go-between   92 *host* lodge; *enjoined penitents* pilgrims bound by oath to their pilgrimage   96 *charge and thanking*
i.e., both expense and gratitude   98 *of* on

III.6 A camp outside Florence   1 *put . . . to't* order him put to the test
(i.e., to fetch his drum)   3 *hilding* base fellow   5 *a bubble* an impostor   8 *as*
as if he were   11–12 *entertainment* maintenance

FIRST LORD   It were fit you knew him, lest reposing too
far in his virtue, which he hath not, he might at some
great and trusty business in a main danger fail you.   15

BERTRAM   I would I knew in what particular action to
try him.

FIRST LORD   None better than to let him fetch off his   18
drum, which you hear him so confidently undertake
to do.   20

SECOND LORD   I with a troop of Florentines will suddenly surprise him; such I will have whom I am sure he
knows not from the enemy. We will bind and hood-   23
wink him so, that he shall suppose no other but that he
is carried into the leaguer of the adversaries when we   25
bring him to our own tents. Be but your lordship present at his examination. If he do not, for the promise of
his life and in the highest compulsion of base fear, offer
to betray you and deliver all the intelligence in his
power against you, and that with the divine forfeit of   30
his soul upon oath, never trust my judgment in anything.

FIRST LORD   O, for the love of laughter, let him fetch his
drum! He says he has a stratagem for't. When your   34
lordship sees the bottom of his success in't, and to what   35
metal this counterfeit lump of ore will be melted, if you
give him not John Drum's entertainment, your inclin-   37
ing cannot be removed. Here he comes.

     Enter Parolles.

SECOND LORD   O, for the love of laughter, hinder not
the honor of his design; let him fetch off his drum in   40
any hand.

BERTRAM   How now, monsieur? This drum sticks sorely   42
in your disposition.

FIRST LORD   A pox on't, let it go! 'tis but a drum.

---

15 *a main danger* an important crisis   18 *fetch off* recapture   23–24 *hoodwink*
blindfold   25 *leaguer* camp   34 *stratagem* plan   35 *bottom* extent   37 *John
Drum's entertainment* unceremonious dismissal (a proverbial expression)
37–38 *inclining* partiality   40–41 *in any hand* in any case   42 *sticks* rankles

PAROLLES   But a drum? Is't but a drum? A drum so lost!
There was excellent command: to charge in with our
47   horse upon our own wings and to rend our own soldiers!

49   FIRST LORD   That was not to be blamed in the command
50   of the service; it was a disaster of war that Caesar himself could not have prevented if he had been there to
command.

53   BERTRAM   Well, we cannot greatly condemn our success.
Some dishonor we had in the loss of that drum, but it
is not to be recovered.

PAROLLES   It might have been recovered.

BERTRAM   It might, but it is not now.

58   PAROLLES   It is to be recovered. But that the merit of service is seldom attributed to the true and exact per-
60   former, I would have that drum or another, or *hic jacet!*

61   BERTRAM   Why, if you have a stomach, to't, monsieur! If
62   you think your mystery in stratagem can bring this in-
63   strument of honor again into his native quarter, be
64   magnanimous in the enterprise and go on; I will grace
65   the attempt for a worthy exploit. If you speed well in it,
the duke shall both speak of it and extend to you what
further becomes his greatness, even to the utmost sylla-
ble of your worthiness.

PAROLLES   By the hand of a soldier, I will undertake it.

70   BERTRAM   But you must not now slumber in it.

71   PAROLLES   I'll about it this evening, and I will presently
72   pen down my dilemmas, encourage myself in my cer-
73   tainty, put myself into my mortal preparation; and by
midnight look to hear further from me.

---

47 *wings* flanks; *rend* attack   49 *in* upon   53 *success* fortune   58 *But that* if
it weren't for the fact that   60 *hic jacet* here lies (i.e., he would die in the attempt)   61 *a stomach* courage   62 *mystery* skill   63 *again . . . quarter* back
home   64 *magnanimous* generous, greathearted; *grace* honor   65 *speed* succeed   70 *you . . . it* i.e., having said so, you must do it expediently   71
presently immediately   72 *pen . . . dilemmas* resolve my doubts   73 *mortal
preparation* (1) preparation to kill others, (2) preparation to meet death

BERTRAM   May I be bold to acquaint his grace you are   75
    gone about it?

PAROLLES   I know not what the success will be, my lord,
    but the attempt I vow.

BERTRAM   I know th' art valiant, and to the possibility of   79
    thy soldiership will subscribe for thee. Farewell.   80

PAROLLES   I love not many words.   *Exit.*

SECOND LORD   No more than a fish loves water. Is not
    this a strange fellow, my lord, that so confidently seems
    to undertake this business, which he knows is not to be
    done; damns himself to do, and dares better be damned   85
    than to do't?

FIRST LORD   You do not know him, my lord, as we do.
    Certain it is that he will steal himself into a man's favor,   88
    and for a week escape a great deal of discoveries; but
    when you find him out, you have him ever after.   90

BERTRAM   Why, do you think he will make no deed at all   91
    of this that so seriously he does address himself unto?

SECOND LORD   None in the world; but return with an
    invention, and clap upon you two or three probable   94
    lies. But we have almost embossed him. You shall see   95
    his fall tonight; for indeed he is not for your lordship's
    respect.

FIRST LORD   We'll make you some sport with the fox ere
    we case him. He was first smoked by the old Lord   99
    Lafew. When his disguise and he is parted, tell me what   100
    a sprat you shall find him, which you shall see this very   101
    night.

SECOND LORD
    I must go look my twigs; he shall be caught.   103

---

75 *his grace* i.e., the duke   79 *possibility* capacity   80 *subscribe for* answer,
vouch for   85 *better* sooner   88 *favor* good graces   90 *have him* have his
measure   91 *deed* attempt   94 *an invention* a tall tale; *probable* plausible
95 *embossed* driven to extremity (used of hunted animals)   99 *case* uncase,
unmask; *smoked* smoked out   101 *sprat* contemptible creature   103 *look my
twigs* look after my traps

BERTRAM
    Your brother, he shall go along with me.
SECOND LORD
    As't please your lordship. I'll leave you.   *[Exit.]*
BERTRAM
    Now will I lead you to the house, and show you
107   The lass I spoke of.
FIRST LORD   But you say she's honest.
BERTRAM
108   That's all the fault. I spoke with her but once
    And found her wondrous cold, but I sent to her,
110   By this same coxcomb that we have i' th' wind,
111   Tokens and letters, which she did resend,
    And this is all I have done. She's a fair creature;
    Will you go see her?
FIRST LORD   With all my heart, my lord.
                              Exeunt.

*

  III.7 *Enter Helena and Widow.*

HELENA
1   If you misdoubt me that I am not she,
    I know not how I shall assure you further
3   But I shall lose the grounds I work upon.
WIDOW
4   Though my estate be fallen, I was well born,
    Nothing acquainted with these businesses,
    And would not put my reputation now
    In any staining act.
HELENA   Nor would I wish you.
    First give me trust the count he is my husband,
    And what to your sworn counsel I have spoken

---

107 *honest* chaste   108 *fault* problem   110 *coxcomb* fool; *that . . . wind*
whom we're hunting   111 *resend* send back
    III.7 The house of a Florentine widow   1 *misdoubt* doubt   3 *But . . .*
upon unless I wreck my plans (by disclosing my identity to Bertram)   4 *es-*
tate condition

Is so from word to word; and then you cannot,   10
By the good aid that I of you shall borrow,   11
Err in bestowing it.
WIDOW   I should believe you,
For you have showed me that which well approves   13
You're great in fortune.
HELENA   Take this purse of gold,
And let me buy your friendly help thus far,
Which I will overpay, and pay again
When I have found it. The count he woos your daugh-
    ter,
Lays down his wanton siege before her beauty,
Resolved to carry her. Let her in fine consent,   19
As we'll direct her how 'tis best to bear it.   *20*
Now his important blood will nought deny   21
That she'll demand. A ring the county wears   22
That downward hath succeeded in his house
From son to son some four or five descents
Since the first father wore it. This ring he holds
In most rich choice; yet in his idle fire,   26
To buy his will, it would not seem too dear,   27
Howe'er repented after.
WIDOW   Now I see
The bottom of your purpose.   29
HELENA
You see it lawful then; it is no more   *30*
But that your daughter, ere she seems as won,
Desires this ring; appoints him an encounter;   32
In fine, delivers me to fill the time,   33
Herself most chastely absent. After,
To marry her, I'll add three thousand crowns   35
To what is passed already.

---

10 *from . . . word* in every detail 11 *By* in respect to 13 *approves* proves
19 *carry her* i.e., seduce her (a military metaphor); *in fine* at length 21 *important* importunate 22 *county* count 26 *most rich choice* highest esteem;
idle careless 27 *will* pleasure 29 *bottom of* intention behind 32 *appoints . . . encounter* makes a rendezvous (with sexual connotation) 33 *to
fill the time* to keep the assignation 35 *To marry her* i.e., by way of dowry

WIDOW   I have yielded.
Instruct my daughter how she shall persever,
That time and place with this deceit so lawful
39   May prove coherent. Every night he comes
40   With musics of all sorts, and songs composed
41   To her unworthiness. It nothing steads us
To chide him from our eaves, for he persists
As if his life lay on't.
HELENA   Why then tonight
44   Let us assay our plot, which if it speed,
45   Is wicked meaning in a lawful deed,
And lawful meaning in a lawful act,
47   Where both not sin, and yet a sinful fact.
But let's about it.   *[Exeunt.]*

                              *

❧ **IV.1** *Enter one of the Frenchmen, [the Second Lord,]*
with five or six other Soldiers, in ambush.

SECOND LORD   He can come no other way but by this
2   hedge corner. When you sally upon him, speak what
3   terrible language you will; though you understand it not
yourselves, no matter; for we must not seem to under-
5   stand him, unless some one among us whom we must
produce for an interpreter.
FIRST SOLDIER   Good captain, let me be th' interpreter.
SECOND LORD   Art not acquainted with him? Knows he
not thy voice?
10   FIRST SOLDIER   No, sir, I warrant you.
11   SECOND LORD   But what linsey-woolsey hast thou to
speak to us again?

---

39 *coherent* in accord   41 *To . . . unworthiness* i.e., to the idea of her sexual
availability; *steads* avails   44 *speed* succeed   45 *meaning* intention   47 *fact*
deed, crime
    IV.1 A field near the camp   2 *sally* rush out   3 *terrible language* terrifying
(but also foreign-sounding) gibberish   5 *unless* except for   10 *warrant* assure   11 *linsey-woolsey* gibberish

FIRST SOLDIER   E'en such as you speak to me.

SECOND LORD   He must think us some band of strangers 14
i' th' adversary's entertainment. Now he hath a smack 15
of all neighboring languages; therefore we must every
one be a man of his own fancy, not to know what we 17
speak one to another; so we seem to know, is to know 18
straight our purpose. Choughs' language – gabble 19
enough, and good enough. As for you, interpreter, you 20
must seem very politic. But couch, ho! Here he comes, 21
to beguile two hours in a sleep, and then to return and 22
swear the lies he forges.   *[They hide.]*
    Enter Parolles.

PAROLLES   Ten o'clock. Within these three hours 'twill be
time enough to go home. What shall I say I have done?
It must be a very plausive invention that carries it. They 26
begin to smoke me, and disgraces have of late knocked 27
too often at my door. I find my tongue is too foolhardy;
but my heart hath the fear of Mars before it, and of his 29
creatures, not daring the reports of my tongue. 30

SECOND LORD   This is the first truth that e'er thine own
tongue was guilty of.

PAROLLES   What the devil should move me to undertake
the recovery of this drum, being not ignorant of the
impossibility, and knowing I had no such purpose? I
must give myself some hurts and say I got them in exploit; yet slight ones will not carry it. They will say, 37
"Came you off with so little?" And great ones I dare not
give. Wherefore, what's the instance? Tongue, I must 39
put you into a butterwoman's mouth, and buy myself 40

---

14 *strangers* foreigners (mercenary soldiers)   15 *entertainment* employ, service; *smack* smattering   17 *of . . . fancy* with a fancied language of his own
18–19 *so . . . purpose* it will suffice if we merely seem to understand each
other   19 *Chough* jackdaw (a kind of crow that can be taught to imitate
human speech)   21 *politic* cunning; *couch, ho* to our hiding places   22 *beguile* while away; *sleep* nap   26 *plausive invention* plausible story; *carries it*
carries it off   27 *smoke* detect   29–30 *his creatures* soldiers   30 *not . . .
tongue* not daring to execute my boasts   37 *carry it* convince   39 *what's the
instance* what is to be the evidence   40 *butterwoman* (a proverbial scold)

41   another of Bajazeth's mule, if you prattle me into these
      perils.

SECOND LORD   Is it possible he should know what he is,
      and be that he is?

PAROLLES   I would the cutting of my garments would
      serve the turn, or the breaking of my Spanish sword.

47 SECOND LORD   We cannot afford you so.

48 PAROLLES   Or the baring of my beard, and to say it was
      in stratagem.

50 SECOND LORD   'Twould not do.

PAROLLES   Or to drown my clothes, and say I was
      stripped.

SECOND LORD   Hardly serve.

PAROLLES   Though I swore I leapt from the window of
      the citadel –

SECOND LORD   How deep?

57 PAROLLES   Thirty fathom.

SECOND LORD   Three great oaths would scarce make that
      be believed.

60 PAROLLES   I would I had any drum of the enemy's; I
      would swear I recovered it.

SECOND LORD   You shall hear one anon.

PAROLLES   A drum now of the enemy's –
      Alarum within.

SECOND LORD   Throca movousus, cargo, cargo, cargo.

ALL   Cargo, cargo, cargo, villianda par corbo, cargo.

PAROLLES
      O, ransom, ransom! Do not hide mine eyes.
      [They blindfold him.]

[FIRST SOLDIER AS] INTERPRETER   Boskos thromuldo
      boskos.

PAROLLES

69   I know you are the Muskos' regiment,

---

41 *another* i.e., another tongue; *Bajazeth's mule* (unexplained, although
mules are notoriously mute)   **47** *afford you so* let you off so easily   **48** *baring* shaving   **57** *fathom* (a measure of six feet)   **69** *Muskos'* Muscovites'

And I shall lose my life for want of language.   70
If there be here German, or Dane, Low Dutch,
Italian, or French, let him speak to me,
I'll discover that which shall undo the Florentine.   73

INTERPRETER   Boskos vauvado. I understand thee, and
can speak thy tongue. Kerelybonto. Sir, betake thee to   75
thy faith, for seventeen poniards are at thy bosom.   76

PAROLLES   O!

INTERPRETER   O, pray, pray, pray! Manka revania dulche.

SECOND LORD   Oscorbidulchos volivorco.

INTERPRETER

The general is content to spare thee yet,   80
And, hoodwinked as thou art, will lead thee on   81
To gather from thee. Haply thou mayst inform   82
Something to save thy life.

PAROLLES   O, let me live,
And all the secrets of our camp I'll show,
Their force, their purposes; nay, I'll speak that
Which you will wonder at.   86

INTERPRETER   But wilt thou faithfully?

PAROLLES

If I do not, damn me.

INTERPRETER

Acordo linta. Come on; thou art granted space.   88
                                    Exit [with Parolles].

    A short alarum within.

SECOND LORD

Go tell the Count Rossillion and my brother,
We have caught the woodcock, and will keep him muf-   90
fled
Till we do hear from them.

SECOND SOLDIER   Captain, I will.

---

70 *want of language* ignorance of your language   73 *discover* reveal; *undo* betray   75–76 *betake . . . faith* i.e., say your prayers   76 *poniards* blades   81
hoodwinked blindfolded   82 *gather* acquire information; *Haply* perhaps   86
faithfully in good faith   88 *space* time   90 *woodcock* (proverbially foolish
bird)

SECOND LORD

92   A will betray us all unto ourselves;

93   Inform on that.

SECOND SOLDIER

                So I will, sir.

SECOND LORD

    Till then I'll keep him dark and safely locked. *Exeunt.*

*

∾ **IV.2** *Enter Bertram and the Maid called Diana.*

BERTRAM

    They told me that your name was Fontybell.

DIANA

    No, my good lord, Diana.

BERTRAM   Titled goddess,

3   And worth it, with addition! But, fair soul,

4   In your fine frame hath love no quality?

5   If the quick fire of youth light not your mind,

6   You are no maiden, but a monument.

    When you are dead you should be such a one

    As you are now, for you are cold and stern;

9   And now you should be as your mother was

10   When your sweet self was got.

DIANA

11   She then was honest.

BERTRAM   So should you be.

DIANA   No.

    My mother did but duty – such, my lord,

    As you owe to your wife.

BERTRAM   No more o' that;

14   I prithee do not strive against my vows.

---

92 *A* he   93 *Inform on* i.e., tell him

    IV.2 The house of a Florentine widow 3 *worth . . . addition* deserving of that title, and more 4 *quality* position 5 *quick* vital 6 *monument* statue 9 *as . . . was* i.e., sexually willing 10 *got* conceived 11 *honest* chaste (because married; Bertram takes it to mean frank or forthcoming) 14 *vows* i.e., those sworn never to be husband to Helena

I was compelled to her, but I love thee   15
By love's own sweet constraint, and will forever
Do thee all rights of service.

DIANA   Ay, so you serve us
Till we serve you; but when you have our roses,   18
You barely leave our thorns to prick ourselves,   19
And mock us with our bareness.   20

BERTRAM   How have I sworn!

DIANA
'Tis not the many oaths that makes the truth,
But the plain single vow that is vowed true.
What is not holy, that we swear not by,
But take the high'st to witness; then pray you tell me,
If I should swear by Jove's great attributes   25
I loved you dearly, would you believe my oaths
When I did love you ill? This has no holding,   27
To swear by him whom I protest to love,   28
That I will work against him. Therefore your oaths   29
Are words, and poor conditions but unsealed –   30
At least in my opinion.

BERTRAM   Change it, change it;
Be not so holy-cruel; love is holy,   32
And my integrity ne'er knew the crafts   33
That you do charge men with. Stand no more off,
But give thyself unto my sick desires,   35
Who then recovers. Say thou art mine, and ever   36
My love, as it begins, shall so persever.   37

DIANA
I see that men may rope's in such a snare   38

---

15 *compelled to her* forced to marry her   18 *serve you* i.e., sexually; *have our roses* i.e., deflower us   19 *prick ourselves* i.e., sting ourselves with remorse (with sexual innuendo of prick as penis)   20 *our bareness* i.e., the loss of our virginity   25 *Jove* king of the Roman gods   27 *ill* poorly or not at all; *holding* binding power   28 *protest* promise   29 *work against him* i.e., contradict the divine law against adultery   30 *poor . . . unsealed* unworthy provisos without binding force (?)   32 *holy-cruel* cruel in your holiness   33 *crafts* deceits   35 *sick* i.e., with longing   36 *Who* i.e., his desire; *ever* forever   37 *persever* continue   38 *rope's* trap us

That we'll forsake ourselves. Give me that ring.

BERTRAM
40 I'll lend it thee, my dear, but have no power
To give it from me.

DIANA   Will you not, my lord?

BERTRAM
42 It is an honor 'longing to our house,
Bequeathèd down from many ancestors,
44 Which were the greatest obloquy i' th' world
45 In me to lose.

DIANA   Mine honor's such a ring;
My chastity's the jewel of our house,
Bequeathèd down from many ancestors,
Which were the greatest obloquy i' th' world
49 In me to lose. Thus your own proper wisdom
50 Brings in the champion Honor on my part
Against your vain assault.

BERTRAM   Here, take my ring!
My house, mine honor, yea, my life be thine,
53 And I'll be bid by thee.

DIANA
When midnight comes, knock at my chamber window;
55 I'll order take my mother shall not hear.
56 Now will I charge you in the band of truth,
When you have conquered my yet maiden bed,
Remain there but an hour, nor speak to me;
My reasons are most strong, and you shall know them
60 When back again this ring shall be delivered.
And on your finger in the night I'll put
62 Another ring, that what in time proceeds
63 May token to the future our past deeds.
Adieu till then; then, fail not; you have won

---

42 *'longing* belonging 44 *obloquy* shame 45 *honor* chastity (with the common bawdy association of *ring* with vagina) 49 *proper* with regard to yourself 50 *champion* defender (as in a chivalric trial by combat); *part* side 53 *bid* commanded 55 *order take* make sure 56 *band* bond 62 *what . . . proceeds* whatever happens 63 *token* (1) betoken, (2) bear witness

A wife of me, though there my hope be done.   65
BERTRAM
A heaven on earth I have won by wooing thee.   *[Exit.]*
DIANA
For which live long to thank both heaven and me!
You may so in the end.
My mother told me just how he would woo,
As if she sat in's heart. She says all men   70
Have the like oaths. He had sworn to marry me
When his wife's dead; therefore I'll lie with him
When I am buried. Since Frenchmen are so braid,   73
Marry that will, I live and die a maid.   74
Only, in this disguise I think't no sin
To cozen him that would unjustly win.   *Exit.*   76

✳

∾ **IV.3** *Enter the two French Captains and some two or*
    three Soldiers.

SECOND LORD   You have not given him his mother's
   letter?
FIRST LORD   I have delivered it an hour since. There is
   something in't that stings his nature, for on the reading
   it he changed almost into another man.
SECOND LORD   He has much worthy blame laid upon   6
   him for shaking off so good a wife and so sweet a lady.
FIRST LORD   Especially he hath incurred the everlasting
   displeasure of the king, who had even tuned his bounty   9
   to sing happiness to him. I will tell you a thing, but you 10
   shall let it dwell darkly with you.   11
SECOND LORD   When you have spoken it, 'tis dead, and I
   am the grave of it.

---

65 *though . . . done* though I thereby forfeit all hope of becoming a wife myself; *done* lost   73 *braid* deceitful   74 *that* who   76 *cozen* cheat
   IV.3 The camp   6 *worthy* deserved   9 *even* accurately; *bounty* generosity
11 *let it dwell darkly* i.e., keep it a secret

FIRST LORD   He hath perverted a young gentlewoman
here in Florence, of a most chaste renown, and this
16   night he fleshes his will in the spoil of her honor. He
17   hath given her his monumental ring, and thinks him-
18   self made in the unchaste composition.

19   SECOND LORD   Now God delay our rebellion! As we are
20   ourselves, what things are we!

21   FIRST LORD   Merely our own traitors. And as in the com-
22   mon course of all treasons, we still see them reveal
23   themselves till they attain to their abhorred ends, so he
24   that in this action contrives against his own nobility, in
his proper stream o'erflows himself.

26   SECOND LORD   Is it not meant damnable in us to be
trumpeters of our unlawful intents? We shall not then
have his company tonight?

29   FIRST LORD   Not till after midnight, for he is dieted to
30   his hour.

SECOND LORD   That approaches apace. I would gladly
32   have him see his company anatomized, that he might
33   take a measure of his own judgments, wherein so curi-
ously he had set this counterfeit.

35   FIRST LORD   We will not meddle with him till he come,
36   for his presence must be the whip of the other.

SECOND LORD   In the meantime, what hear you of these
wars?

FIRST LORD   I hear there is an overture of peace.

40   SECOND LORD   Nay, I assure you, a peace concluded.

---

16 *fleshes his will* gratifies his lust; *spoil* ruin; *honor* chastity   17 *monumental*
serving as a token of identity   18 *unchaste composition* dishonorable bargain
19 *delay* mitigate; *rebellion* outbreaks of lust   20 *ourselves* i.e., unaided by
heaven   21 *Merely* entirely   22 *still* always   22–23 *reveal themselves* i.e., for
what they are   23 *attain . . . ends* reach their abhorrent conclusions (i.e.,
self-destruction)   24 *contrives* plots   24–25 *in . . . himself* undoes his own
nobility with his own plots   26 *meant damnable* a sign of damnation   29
dieted restricted   32 *company* companion (i.e., Parolles); *anatomized* laid
bare, exposed   33 *take . . . judgments* appreciate his own misjudgment
33–34 *so . . . counterfeit* so elaborately he had set this false jewel   35 *him*
Parolles; *he* Bertram   36 *his* Bertram's; *the other* Parolles

FIRST LORD   What will Count Rossillion do then? Will
he travel higher, or return again into France?   42

SECOND LORD   I perceive by this demand you are not altogether of his council.   44

FIRST LORD   Let it be forbid, sir! So should I be a great
deal of his act.   46

SECOND LORD   Sir, his wife some two months since fled
from his house. Her pretense is a pilgrimage to Saint   48
Jaques le Grand; which holy undertaking with most
austere sanctimony she accomplished; and there resid-   50
ing, the tenderness of her nature became as a prey to
her grief; in fine, made a groan of her last breath, and   52
now she sings in heaven.

FIRST LORD   How is this justified?   54

SECOND LORD   The stronger part of it by her own letters,   55
which makes her story true, even to the point of her   56
death. Her death itself, which could not be her office to   57
say is come, was faithfully confirmed by the rector of   58
the place.

FIRST LORD   Hath the count all this intelligence?   60

SECOND LORD   Ay, and the particular confirmations,
point from point, to the full arming of the verity.   62

FIRST LORD   I am heartily sorry that he'll be glad of this.

SECOND LORD   How mightily sometimes we make us
comforts of our losses!

FIRST LORD   And how mightily some other times we
drown our gain in tears! The great dignity that his valor   67
hath here acquired for him shall at home be encoun-
tered with a shame as ample.

SECOND LORD   The web of our life is of a mingled yarn,   70
good and ill together; our virtues would be proud if our

---

42 *higher* farther   44 *of his council* in his confidence   46 *of his act* answer-
able for his actions   48 *pretense* intent   50 *sanctimony* holiness   52 *in fine*
at last   54 *justified* verified   55 *stronger* larger   56 *point* moment   57–58
which . . . come which she could not herself report   58 *rector* ruler   62 *arming* corroboration; *verity* truth   67 *gain* profits

faults whipped them not, and our crimes would despair
73   if they were not cherished by our virtues.
      Enter a Messenger.
      How now? Where's your master?

MESSENGER   He met the duke in the street, sir, of whom
76   he hath taken a solemn leave; his lordship will next
      morning for France. The duke hath offered him letters
      of commendations to the king.   *[Exit.]*

79   FIRST LORD   They shall be no more than needful there, if
80   they were more than they can commend.
      Enter [Bertram] Count Rossillion.

SECOND LORD   They cannot be too sweet for the king's
      tartness. Here's his lordship now. How now, my lord,
      is't not after midnight?

BERTRAM   I have tonight dispatched sixteen businesses, a
85   month's length apiece. By an abstract of success: I have
86   congied with the duke, done my adieu with his nearest,
      buried a wife, mourned for her, writ to my lady mother
88   I am returning, entertained my convoy, and between
89   these main parcels of dispatch effected many nicer
90   needs. The last was the greatest, but that I have not
      ended yet.

SECOND LORD   If the business be of any difficulty, and
      this morning your departure hence, it requires haste of
      your lordship.

95   BERTRAM   I mean the business is not ended, as fearing to
      hear of it hereafter. But shall we have this dialogue be-
      tween the fool and the soldier? Come, bring forth this
98   counterfeit module has deceived me like a double-
      meaning prophesier.

---

73 *cherished* countered   76 *will* will make, depart   79 *no . . . needful* i.e., of
the utmost necessity   79–80 *if . . . commend* even if they outdid all possible
commendation   85 *By . . . success* to enumerate my successes   86 *congied
with* taken leave of; *his nearest* his companions   88 *entertained my convoy*
arranged my transportation   89 *parcels of dispatch* items of business; *nicer*
more delicate   90 *The last* i.e., the assignation with Diana   95–96 *as . . .
hear* since I fear I may hear   98 *module* mere image   98–99 *double-meaning*
equivocating

SECOND LORD   Bring him forth. *[Exeunt Soldiers.]* Has   *100*
sat i' th' stocks all night, poor gallant knave.

BERTRAM   No matter, his heels have deserved it, in
usurping his spurs so long. How does he carry himself?

SECOND LORD   I have told your lordship already: the
stocks carry him. But to answer you as you would be
understood, he weeps like a wench that had shed her   *106*
milk; he hath confessed himself to Morgan, whom he
supposes to be a friar, from the time of his remem-   *108*
brance to this very instant disaster of his setting i' th'   *109*
stocks. And what think you he hath confessed?   *110*

BERTRAM   Nothing of me, has a?   *111*

SECOND LORD   His confession is taken, and it shall be
read to his face. If your lordship be in't, as I believe you
are, you must have the patience to hear it.

  Enter Parolles [guarded,] with [First Soldier as] his
  Interpreter.

BERTRAM   A plague upon him! muffled! He can say   *115*
nothing of me.

FIRST LORD   Hush, hush! Hoodman comes! Portotar-   *117*
tarossa.

INTERPRETER   He calls for the tortures; what will you say
without 'em?   *120*

PAROLLES   I will confess what I know without constraint.
If ye pinch me like a pasty, I can say no more.   *122*

INTERPRETER   Bosko chimurcho.

FIRST LORD   Boblibindo chicurmurco.

INTERPRETER   You are a merciful general. Our general
bids you answer to what I shall ask you out of a note.   *126*

PAROLLES   And truly, as I hope to live.

INTERPRETER   *[Reads.]* "First demand of him how many
horse the duke is strong." What say you to that?   *129*

---

106 *shed* spilled   **108–9** *time . . . remembrance* as far back as he can remember   **109** *instant* present   **111** *a* he   **115** *muffled* blindfolded   **117** *Hoodman comes* (a standard cry in the game of blindman's buff)   **122** *pasty* meat
pie   **126** *note* memorandum   **129** *horse* cavalry troops

130 PAROLLES   Five or six thousand, but very weak and un-
serviceable. The troops are all scattered, and the com-
manders very poor rogues, upon my reputation and
credit, and as I hope to live.

INTERPRETER   Shall I set down your answer so?

PAROLLES   Do. I'll take the sacrament on't, how and
which way you will.

137 BERTRAM   All's one to him. What a past-saving slave is
this!

FIRST LORD   You're deceived, my lord. This is Monsieur
140 Parolles, the gallant militarist – that was his own
141 phrase – that had the whole theoric of war in the knot
142 of his scarf, and the practice in the chape of his dagger.

SECOND LORD   I will never trust a man again for keeping
his sword clean, nor believe he can have everything in
145 him by wearing his apparel neatly.

INTERPRETER   Well, that's set down.

PAROLLES   "Five or six thousand horse," I said – I will say
true – "or thereabouts" set down, for I'll speak truth.

FIRST LORD   He's very near the truth in this.

150 BERTRAM   But I con him no thanks for't, in the nature he
delivers it.

PAROLLES   "Poor rogues," I pray you say.

INTERPRETER   Well, that's set down.

PAROLLES   I humbly thank you, sir; a truth's a truth – the
155 rogues are marvelous poor.

INTERPRETER   *[Reads.]* "Demand of him of what
strength they are afoot." What say you to that?

158 PAROLLES   By my troth, sir, if I were to live this present
hour, I will tell true. Let me see: Spurio, a hundred and
160 fifty; Sebastian, so many; Corambus, so many; Jaques,
so many; Guiltian, Cosmo, Lodowick, and Gratii, two
hundred fifty each; mine own company, Chitopher,

---

137 *past-saving* damned   141 *theoric* theory   142 *chape* tip of the scabbard
145 *neatly* elegantly   150 *con* offer; *in the nature* considering the manner
155 *marvelous* remarkably   158–59 *if . . . hour* if I had but this one hour to
live

Vaumond, Bentii, two hundred fifty each; so that the
muster file, rotten and sound, upon my life amounts   164
not to fifteen thousand poll, half of the which dare not   165
shake the snow from off their cassocks, lest they shake   166
themselves to pieces.

BERTRAM   What shall be done to him?

FIRST LORD   Nothing, but let him have thanks. Demand
of him my condition, and what credit I have with the   *170*
duke.

INTERPRETER   Well, that's set down. *[Reads.]* "You shall
demand of him whether one Captain Dumaine be i' th'
camp, a Frenchman; what his reputation is with the
duke; what his valor, honesty, and expertness in wars;
or whether he thinks it were not possible, with well-   176
weighing sums of gold, to corrupt him to a revolt."
What say you to this? What do you know of it?

PAROLLES   I beseech you let me answer to the particular
of the inter'gatories. Demand them singly.   180

INTERPRETER   Do you know this Captain Dumaine?

PAROLLES   I know him. A was a botcher's prentice in   182
Paris, from whence he was whipped for getting the
shrieve's fool with child – a dumb innocent, that could   184
not say him nay.

[First Lord makes as if to strike him.]

BERTRAM   Nay, by your leave, hold your hands, though I
know his brains are forfeit to the next tile that falls.   187

INTERPRETER   Well, is this captain in the Duke of Florence's camp?

PAROLLES   Upon my knowledge he is, and lousy.   190

FIRST LORD   Nay, look not so upon me; we shall hear of
your lordship anon.   192

INTERPRETER   What is his reputation with the duke?

---

164 *file* roll   165 *poll* heads   166 *cassocks* cloaks   176–77 *well-weighing* (1)
heavy, (2) apt to influence   180 *inter'gatories* questions   182 *A* he; *botcher*
cobbler, tailor   184 *shrieve's fool* feebleminded man in the sheriff's custody;
innocent mental defective   187 *his . . . falls* he's in danger of death at any
moment   190 *lousy* (1) incompetent, (2) lice-infested   192 *anon* soon

PAROLLES   The duke knows him for no other but a poor
officer of mine, and writ to me this other day to turn
196   him out o' th' band. I think I have his letter in my
pocket.

INTERPRETER   Marry, we'll search.

199   PAROLLES   In good sadness, I do not know; either it is
200   there, or it is upon a file with the duke's other letters in
my tent.

INTERPRETER   Here 'tis; here's a paper; shall I read it to
you?

PAROLLES   I do not know if it be it or no.

BERTRAM   Our interpreter does it well.

FIRST LORD   Excellently.

INTERPRETER   *[Reads.]*
"Dian, the count's a fool, and full of gold."

208   PAROLLES   That is not the duke's letter, sir; that is an ad-
209   vertisement to a proper maid in Florence, one Diana,
210   to take heed of the allurement of one Count Rossillion,
211   a foolish idle boy, but for all that very ruttish. I pray
212   you, sir, put it up again.

INTERPRETER   Nay, I'll read it first, by your favor.

PAROLLES   My meaning in't, I protest, was very honest in
the behalf of the maid; for I knew the young count to
be a dangerous and lascivious boy, who is a whale to
217   virginity, and devours up all the fry it finds.

218   BERTRAM   Damnable both-sides rogue!

INTERPRETER   *[Reads.]*
"When he swears oaths, bid him drop gold, and take it;
220   After he scores, he never pays the score.
221   Half-won is match well made; match, and well make it;
222   He ne'er pays after-debts, take it before.
And say a soldier, Dian, told thee this:

---

196 *his* i.e., the duke's   199 *sadness* earnest   200 *upon* in   208–9 *advertise-ment* warning   209 *proper* respectable   211 *ruttish* lecherous   212 *up* away   217 *fry* unsuspecting victims (literally, small fish)   218 *both-sides* double-crossing   220 *scores* buys on credit; *score* reckoning   221 *match well made* bargain well concluded   222 *after-debts* debts payable after the transaction is complete; *it* i.e., Bertram's gold

Men are to mell with, boys are not to kiss.   224
For count of this, the count's a fool, I know it,   225
Who pays before, but not when he does owe it,   226
      Thine, as he vowed to thee in thine ear,
                    Parolles."

BERTRAM   He shall be whipped through the army with
this rhyme in's forehead.   230

SECOND LORD   This is your devoted friend, sir, the man-   231
ifold linguist and the armipotent soldier.   232

BERTRAM   I could endure anything before but a cat, and   233
now he's a cat to me.

INTERPRETER   I perceive, sir, by the general's looks, we
shall be fain to hang you.   236

PAROLLES   My life, sir, in any case! Not that I am afraid
to die, but that my offenses being many, I would repent
out the remainder of nature. Let me live, sir, in a dun-   239
geon, i' th' stocks, or anywhere, so I may live.   240

INTERPRETER   We'll see what may be done, so you confess freely. Therefore, once more to this Captain Dumaine: you have answered to his reputation with the
duke and to his valor. What is his honesty?

PAROLLES   He will steal, sir, an egg out of a cloister. For
rapes and ravishments he parallels Nessus. He professes   246
not keeping of oaths; in breaking 'em he is stronger
than Hercules. He will lie, sir, with such volubility that   248
you would think truth were a fool; drunkenness is his
best virtue, for he will be swine-drunk, and in his sleep   250
he does little harm, save to his bedclothes about him;   251
but they know his conditions and lay him in straw. I   252
have but little more to say, sir, of his honesty: he has

---

224 *mell* have sexual intercourse   225 *count of* attend to   226 *before* in ad-
vance; *owe* (1) owe payment, (2) possess (own) her virginity   231–32 *manifold* multiple   232 *armipotent* mighty in arms   233 *cat* spiteful or
backbiting person (usually applied to women)   236 *fain* obliged   239 *remainder of nature* rest of my natural life   246 *Nessus* the centaur (half man,
half horse) who tried to rape Hercules' wife   246–47 *professes not* does not
make a practice of   248 *volubility* fluency   251 *save to his bedclothes* i.e., he
wets the bed   252 *they* i.e., other people; *conditions* disposition

everything that an honest man should not have; what
an honest man should have, he has nothing.

FIRST LORD   I begin to love him for this.

BERTRAM   For this description of thine honesty? A pox
upon him! For me, he's more and more a cat.

INTERPRETER   What say you to his expertness in war?

260 PAROLLES   Faith, sir, has led the drum before the English
tragedians – to belie him I will not – and more of his
soldiership I know not, except in that country he had
263 the honor to be the officer at a place there called Mile
264 End, to instruct for the doubling of files. I would do
265 the man what honor I can, but of this I am not certain.

FIRST LORD   He hath outvillained villainy so far that the
267 rarity redeems him.

BERTRAM   A pox on him! He's a cat still.

269 INTERPRETER   His qualities being at this poor price, I
270 need not to ask you if gold will corrupt him to revolt.

271 PAROLLES   Sir, for a cardecue he will sell the fee simple of
272 his salvation, the inheritance of it, and cut th' entail
273 from all remainders, and a perpetual succession for it
perpetually.

INTERPRETER   What's his brother, the other Captain Dumaine?

SECOND LORD   Why does he ask him of me?

INTERPRETER   What's he?

PAROLLES   E'en a crow o' th' same nest; not altogether so
280 great as the first in goodness, but greater a great deal in
evil. He excels his brother for a coward, yet his brother
is reputed one of the best that is. In a retreat he outruns
283 any lackey; marry, in coming on he has the cramp.

260–61 *led . . . tragedians* banged a drum to help advertise plays   263–64
Mile End (field in London where citizen recruits were drilled)   264 *the doubling of files* simple drill maneuvers   265 *this* i.e., his service at Mile End
267 *rarity* extravagant accomplishment   269 *qualities* virtues, abilities   271
cardecue i.e., *quart d'écu*, a small French coin; *fee simple* absolute and perpetual ownership   272 *entail* succession   273 *remainders* possible future heirs
283 *lackey* running footman; *marry* indeed; *coming on* advancing, attacking

INTERPRETER   If your life be saved, will you undertake to
betray the Florentine?

PAROLLES   Ay, and the captain of his horse, Count
Rossillion.

INTERPRETER   I'll whisper with the general, and know
his pleasure.

PAROLLES   *[Aside]* I'll no more drumming; a plague of all   *290*
drums! Only to seem to deserve well, and to beguile the   *291*
supposition of that lascivious young boy, the count,
have I run into this danger; yet who would have suspected an ambush where I was taken?

INTERPRETER   There is no remedy, sir, but you must die.
The general says, you that have so traitorously discov-   *296*
ered the secrets of your army, and made such pestifer-   *297*
ous reports of men very nobly held, can serve the world   *298*
for no honest use; therefore you must die. Come,
headsman, off with his head!   *300*

PAROLLES

O Lord, sir, let me live, or let me see my death!

INTERPRETER

That shall you, and take your leave of all your friends.
    [Unmuffles him.]
So, look about you. Know you any here?

BERTRAM   Good morrow, noble captain.

SECOND LORD   God bless you, Captain Parolles.

FIRST LORD   God save you, noble captain.

SECOND LORD   Captain, what greeting will you to my
Lord Lafew? I am for France.

FIRST LORD   Good captain, will you give me a copy of
the sonnet you writ to Diana in behalf of the Count   *310*
Rossillion? An I were not a very coward, I'd compel it   *311*
of you; but fare you well.   *Exeunt [Bertram and Lords].*

INTERPRETER   You are undone, captain – all but your
scarf; that has a knot on't yet.

291–92 *beguile the supposition* deceive the judgment   **296–97** *discovered* dis-
closed   **297–98** *pestiferous* mischievous   **298** *held* esteemed   **311** *An* if;
very perfect

315 PAROLLES Who cannot be crushed with a plot?

INTERPRETER   If you could find out a country where but
women were that had received so much shame, you
might begin an impudent nation. Fare ye well, sir; I am
for France too; we shall speak of you there.

Exit [with Soldiers].

PAROLLES
320   Yet am I thankful. If my heart were great,
'Twould burst at this. Captain I'll be no more,
But I will eat and drink and sleep as soft
As captain shall. Simply the thing I am
324   Shall make me live. Who knows himself a braggart,
Let him fear this; for it will come to pass
That every braggart shall be found an ass.
Rust, sword! cool, blushes! and, Parolles, live
328   Safest in shame; being fooled, by foolery thrive.
There's place and means for every man alive.
330   I'll after them.   *Exit.*

*

❧ **IV.4** *Enter Helena, Widow, and Diana.*

HELENA
That you may well perceive I have not wronged you,
One of the greatest in the Christian world
3   Shall be my surety; 'fore whose throne 'tis needful,
Ere I can perfect mine intents, to kneel.
Time was I did him a desirèd office,
6   Dear almost as his life; which gratitude
Through flinty Tartar's bosom would peep forth
And answer thanks. I duly am informed
9   His grace is at Marseilles, to which place
10   We have convenient convoy. You must know

---

315 *a plot* treachery   **324** *Who* he who   **328** *fooled* proved a fool; *foolery* folly
   IV.4 The house of a Florentine widow   **3** *surety* guarantee   **6** *which gratitude* gratitude for which   **9** *Marseilles* (a trisyllable, spelled "Marcellae" in the folio)   **10** *convoy* escort, transportation

I am supposèd dead; the army breaking,   11
My husband hies him home, where, heaven aiding,
And by the leave of my good lord the king,
We'll be before our welcome.   14
WIDOW   Gentle madam,
You never had a servant to whose trust
Your business was more welcome.
HELENA   Nor you, mistress,
Ever a friend whose thoughts more truly labor
To recompense your love. Doubt not but heaven
Hath brought me up to be your daughter's dower,
As it hath fated her to be my motive   20
And helper to a husband. But, O strange men!
That can such sweet use make of what they hate,
When saucy trusting of the cozened thoughts   23
Defiles the pitchy night; so lust doth play
With what it loathes, for that which is away.   25
But more of this hereafter. You, Diana,
Under my poor instructions yet must suffer
Something in my behalf.   28
DIANA   Let death and honesty
Go with your impositions, I am yours
Upon your will to suffer.   30
HELENA   Yet, I pray you.
But with the word the time will bring on summer,   31
When briers shall have leaves as well as thorns,
And be as sweet as sharp. We must away;
Our wagon is prepared, and time revives us.   34
All's well that ends well; still the fine's the crown.   35
Whate'er the course, the end is the renown.   *Exeunt.*

                          *

_____

11 *breaking* disbanding   14 *be before* arrive ahead of   20 *motive* means,
agent (?)   23–24 *When . . . night* when wanton yielding to the deceptions of
lust makes black night even blacker   25 *for* in place of   28–30 *Let . . . suffer* so long as your instructions allow me to preserve my chastity, I am ready
to die at your command   30 *Yet* a while longer   31 *with the word* only with
the saying of it (?)   34 *wagon* carriage   35 *fine* end

~ **IV.5** *Enter [Lavatch, the] Clown, Old Lady*
   [Countess], and Lafew.

1 LAFEW   No, no, no, your son was misled with a snipped-
2   taffeta fellow there, whose villainous saffron would
3   have made all the unbaked and doughy youth of a na-
    tion in his color. Your daughter-in-law had been alive at
    this hour, and your son here at home, more advanced
6   by the king than by that red-tailed humblebee I speak
    of.

   COUNTESS   I would I had not known him; it was the
    death of the most virtuous gentlewoman that ever na-
10 ture had praise for creating. If she had partaken of my
11 flesh and cost me the dearest groans of a mother, I
12 could not have owed her a more rooted love.

   LAFEW   'Twas a good lady, 'twas a good lady. We may
14 pick a thousand sallets ere we light on such another
    herb.

   LAVATCH   Indeed, sir, she was the sweet marjoram of the
17 sallet, or rather, the herb of grace.

18 LAFEW   They are not herbs, you knave; they are nose
    herbs.

20 LAVATCH   I am no great Nebuchadnezzar, sir; I have not
21 much skill in grass.

22 LAFEW   Whether dost thou profess thyself, a knave or a
    fool?

   LAVATCH   A fool, sir, at a woman's service, and a knave at
    a man's.

   LAFEW   Your distinction?

IV.5 The palace of the Countess of Rossillion   **1–2** *snipped-taffeta* slashed
silk, both gaudy and flimsy   **2** *saffron* yellow dye   **3** *unbaked* i.e., half-
baked; *doughy* raw   **6** *red-tailed* i.e., brightly colored   **11** *dearest groans*
direst childbirth pains   **12** *rooted* established, firm   **14** *sallets* salads   **17** *the*
herb of grace rue   **18** *not herbs* not edible plants   **18–19** *nose herbs* aromatic
plants   **20** *Nebuchadnezzar* Babylonian king who went mad and ate grass
(Daniel 4:28–37)   **21** *grass* (with pun on "grace")   **22** *Whether* which

LAVATCH   I would cozen the man of his wife, and do his   27
service.

LAFEW   So you were a knave at his service indeed.

LAVATCH   And I would give his wife my bauble, sir, to do   30
her service.

LAFEW   I will subscribe for thee, thou art both knave and   32
fool.

LAVATCH   At your service.

LAFEW   No, no, no!   35

LAVATCH   Why, sir, if I cannot serve you, I can serve as
great a prince as you are.

LAFEW   Who's that? a Frenchman?

LAVATCH   Faith, sir, a has an English name, but his fis-   39
nomy is more hotter in France than there.   40

LAFEW   What prince is that?

LAVATCH   The Black Prince, sir, alias the prince of dark-   42
ness, alias the devil.

LAFEW   Hold thee, there's my purse. I give thee not this
to suggest thee from thy master thou talk'st of; serve   45
him still.   46

LAVATCH   I am a woodland fellow, sir, that always loved a   47
great fire, and the master I speak of ever keeps a good
fire. But sure he is the prince of the world; let his nobility remain in's court; I am for the house with the nar-   50
row gate, which I take to be too little for pomp to enter.
Some that humble themselves may, but the many will   52
be too chill and tender, and they'll be for the flowery   53
way that leads to the broad gate and the great fire.

LAFEW   Go thy ways; I begin to be aweary of thee; and I   55

---

27 *cozen* cheat   27–28 *do his service* take his place sexually   30 *my bauble* a
stick carried by a court jester (with sexual innuendo)   32 *subscribe* vouch
35 *No, no, no* (Lafew has no intention of accepting Lavatch's service as either
knave or fool)   39 *a* he   39–40 *fisnomy* physiognomy   42 *Black Prince*
(nickname of the eldest son of Edward III, hence the *English name* of l. 39)
45 *suggest* lure   46 *still* ever   47 *woodland* rustic   50–51 *narrow gate* i.e.,
the righteous path (Matthew 7:13–14)   52 *many* multitude   53 *chill and
tender* susceptible to cold   55 *Go thy ways* get along

56   tell thee so before, because I would not fall out with
      thee. Go thy ways; let my horses be well looked to,
      without any tricks.

      LAVATCH   If I put any tricks upon 'em, sir, they shall be
60   jades' tricks, which are their own right by the law of na-
      ture.   *Exit.*

62   LAFEW   A shrewd knave and an unhappy.

      COUNTESS   So a is. My lord that's gone made himself
      much sport out of him. By his authority he remains
      here, which he thinks is a patent for his sauciness; and
66   indeed he has no pace, but runs where he will.

      LAFEW   I like him well; 'tis not amiss. And I was about to
      tell you, since I heard of the good lady's death, and that
      my lord your son was upon his return home, I moved
70   the king my master to speak in the behalf of my daugh-
      ter; which, in the minority of them both, his majesty
72   out of a self-gracious remembrance did first propose.
73   His highness hath promised me to do it; and to stop up
      the displeasure he hath conceived against your son
      there is no fitter matter. How does your ladyship like it?

      COUNTESS   With very much content, my lord, and I
      wish it happily effected.

78   LAFEW   His highness comes post from Marseilles, of as
79   able body as when he numbered thirty; a will be here
80   tomorrow, or I am deceived by him that in such intelli-
      gence hath seldom failed.

      COUNTESS   It rejoices me that I hope I shall see him ere I
      die. I have letters that my son will be here tonight. I
      shall beseech your lordship to remain with me till they
      meet together.

      LAFEW   Madam, I was thinking with what manners I
87   might safely be admitted.

---

56 *before* beforehand   60 *jades' tricks* mischievous tricks (played by recalcitrant horses)   62 *shrewd* sharp-tongued   66 *has no pace* is unrestrained   72
a self-gracious remembrance unprompted generosity   73 *stop up* plug (like a
pipeline)   78 *post* posthaste, quickly   79 *numbered thirty* was thirty years
old   80 *him* his messenger   87 *admitted* i.e., (1) to the meeting, (2) to the
countess's residence

COUNTESS   You need but plead your honorable privilege.   88
LAFEW   Lady, of that I have made a bold charter, but I   89
thank my God it holds yet.   90
        Enter [Lavatch, the] Clown.
LAVATCH   O madam, yonder's my lord your son with a
patch of velvet on's face. Whether there be a scar under't or no, the velvet knows, but 'tis a goodly patch of
velvet; his left cheek is a cheek of two pile and a half,   94
but his right cheek is worn bare.   95
LAFEW   A scar nobly got, or a noble scar, is a good livery
of honor; so belike is that.   97
LAVATCH   But it is your carbonadoed face.   98
LAFEW   Let us go see your son, I pray you. I long to talk
with the young noble soldier.   100
LAVATCH   Faith, there's a dozen of 'em, with delicate fine
hats, and most courteous feathers which bow the head
and nod at every man.   *Exeunt.*
                            *

∾ **V.1** *Enter Helena, Widow, and Diana, with two
Attendants.*

HELENA
    But this exceeding posting day and night   1
    Must wear your spirits low. We cannot help it;
    But since you have made the days and nights as one,
    To wear your gentle limbs in my affairs,   4
    Be bold you do so grow in my requital   5
    As nothing can unroot you.   6
        Enter a Gentleman.
                        In happy time –

---

88 *honorable privilege* privilege due your honor 89 *made . . . charter* exploited my license as far as possible 94 *two . . . half* especially thick velvet
95 *worn bare* unpatched 97 *belike* probably 98 *carbonadoed* slashed (to
drain venereal ulcers)
    V.1 A street in Marseilles 1 *posting* riding 4 *wear* wear out, tire 5 *bold*
assured; *requital* thankfulness 6 *happy time* good timing (said of the gentleman's arrival)

This man may help me to his majesty's ear,
8   If he would spend his power. God save you, sir!
GENTLEMAN
    And you.
HELENA
10   Sir, I have seen you in the court of France.
GENTLEMAN
    I have been sometimes there.
HELENA
    I do presume, sir, that you are not fall'n
    From the report that goes upon your goodness;
14   And therefore, goaded with most sharp occasions,
15   Which lay nice manners by, I put you to
    The use of your own virtues, for the which
    I shall continue thankful.
GENTLEMAN   What's your will?
HELENA
    That it will please you
    To give this poor petition to the king,
20   And aid me with that store of power you have
    To come into his presence.
GENTLEMAN
    The king's not here.
HELENA   Not here, sir?
GENTLEMAN   Not indeed;
23   He hence removed last night, and with more haste
24   Than is his use.
WIDOW   Lord, how we lose our pains!
HELENA
    All's well that ends well yet,
    Though time seem so adverse and means unfit.
    I do beseech you, whither is he gone?
GENTLEMAN
    Marry, as I take it, to Rossillion,

---

8 *spend* expend   14 *sharp* pressing   15 *nice* scrupulous; *put* urge   **15–16**
I . . . virtues I help you put your goodness into action   23 *hence removed* left
here   24 *use* wont, habit

Whither I am going.

HELENA   I do beseech you, sir,
Since you are like to see the king before me,   30
Commend the paper to his gracious hand,   31
Which I presume shall render you no blame,
But rather make you thank your pains for it.
I will come after you with what good speed
Our means will make us means.   35

GENTLEMAN   This I'll do for you.

HELENA
And you shall find yourself to be well thanked,
Whate'er falls more. – We must to horse again.   37
Go, go, provide.   *[Exeunt.]*

                          *

∞ **V.2** *Enter [Lavatch, the] Clown, and Parolles.*

PAROLLES   Good Master Lavatch, give my Lord Lafew
this letter. I have ere now, sir, been better known to
you, when I have held familiarity with fresher clothes;
but I am now, sir, muddied in Fortune's mood, and   4
smell somewhat strong of her strong displeasure.

LAVATCH   Truly, Fortune's displeasure is but sluttish if it
smell so strongly as thou speak'st of; I will henceforth
eat no fish of Fortune's butt'ring. Prithee, allow the   8
wind!

PAROLLES   Nay, you need not to stop your nose, sir; I   10
spake but by a metaphor.

LAVATCH   Indeed, sir, if your metaphor stink, I will stop
my nose, or against any man's metaphor. Prithee, get
thee further.

PAROLLES   Pray you, sir, deliver me this paper.

---

31 *Commend* deliver   35 *Our means . . . means* our resources will permit
37 *falls more* else falls out, else results
    V.2 The palace of the Countess of Rossillion   4 *mood* anger   8 *of Fortune's butt'ring* served up by Fortune   8–9 *allow the wind* stand downwind

LAVATCH   Foh! prithee, stand away! A paper from For-
17   tune's closestool, to give to a nobleman! Look, here he
comes himself.
    Enter Lafew.
19   Here is a pur of Fortune's, sir, or of Fortune's cat – but
20   not a musk cat – that has fallen into the unclean fish
pond of her displeasure, and, as he says, is muddied
22   withal. Pray you, sir, use the carp as you may, for he
23   looks like a poor decayed, ingenious, foolish, rascally
knave. I do pity his distress in my similes of comfort,
and leave him to your lordship.   *[Exit.]*

PAROLLES   My lord, I am a man whom Fortune hath cru-
elly scratched.

LAFEW   And what would you have me to do? 'Tis too late
to pare her nails now. Wherein have you played the
30   knave with Fortune that she should scratch you, who of
herself is a good lady, and would not have knaves thrive
32   long under her? There's a cardecue for you. Let the justices make you and Fortune friends; I am for other
business.

PAROLLES   I beseech your honor to hear me one single
word.

LAFEW   You beg a single penny more. Come, you shall
ha't; save your word.

PAROLLES   My name, my good lord, is Parolles.

40   LAFEW   You beg more than word then. Cox my passion!
Give me your hand. How does your drum?

42   PAROLLES   O my good lord, you were the first that found
me.

44   LAFEW   Was I, in sooth? And I was the first that lost thee.

---

17 *closestool* privy   19 *pur* knave (the jack in cards, with pun on "purr")   20
musk cat (prized for its scent); *unclean* (household waste was often emptied
into ponds where fish were raised for food)   22 *carp* (inhabitant of *unclean
fish pond,* and a proverbial chatterer)   23 *ingenious* inept (?)   32 *cardecue*
i.e., *quart d'écu,* a French coin   32–33 *justices* (under Elizabethan law, responsible for beggars)   40 *more than word* i.e., many words, "Parolles"; *Cox*
God's   42–43 *found me* found me out   44 *lost* disdained, deserted

PAROLLES   It lies in you, my lord, to bring me in some
grace, for you did bring me out.

LAFEW   Out upon thee, knave! Dost thou put upon me
at once both the office of God and the devil? One
brings thee in grace, and the other brings thee out.
[Trumpets sound.] The king's coming; I know by his   50
trumpets. Sirrah, inquire further after me; I had talk of
you last night; though you are a fool and a knave, you
shall eat. Go to; follow.

PAROLLES   I praise God for you.   *[Exeunt.]*

                         *

∽ **V.3** *Flourish. Enter King, Old Lady [Countess],*
      Lafew, the two French Lords, with Attendants.

KING

We lost a jewel of her, and our esteem   1
Was made much poorer by it; but your son,
As mad in folly, lacked the sense to know   3
Her estimation home.

COUNTESS   'Tis past, my liege,
And I beseech your majesty to make it
Natural rebellion, done i' th' blade of youth,   6
When oil and fire, too strong for reason's force,
O'erbears it and burns on.

KING   My honored lady,
I have forgiven and forgotten all,
Though my revenges were high bent upon him,   10
And watched the time to shoot.   11

LAFEW   This I must say —
But first I beg my pardon — the young lord
Did to his majesty, his mother, and his lady,

V.3 The palace of the Countess of Rossillion   **1** *our esteem* our own value
3–4 *know . . . home* appreciate her worth to the full   **6** *blade* i.e., immaturity, greenness   **10** *high bent* aimed like a fully drawn bow   **11** *watched the
time* waited for the right moment

Offense of mighty note, but to himself
The greatest wrong of all. He lost a wife
16 Whose beauty did astonish the survey
17 Of richest eyes, whose words all ears took captive,
Whose dear perfection hearts that scorned to serve
Humbly called mistress.

KING   Praising what is lost
20 Makes the remembrance dear. Well, call him hither;
We are reconciled, and the first view shall kill
22 All repetition. Let him not ask our pardon;
23 The nature of his great offense is dead,
And deeper than oblivion we do bury
25 Th' incensing relics of it. Let him approach,
A stranger, no offender; and inform him
So 'tis our will he should.

GENTLEMAN   I shall, my liege.   *[Exit.]*

KING
What says he to your daughter? Have you spoke?

LAFEW
29 All that he is hath reference to your highness.

KING
30 Then shall we have a match. I have letters sent me
That sets him high in fame.
        Enter Count Bertram.

LAFEW   He looks well on't.

KING
32 I am not a day of season,
For thou mayst see a sunshine and a hail
In me at once. But to the brightest beams
Distracted clouds give way; so stand thou forth,
The time is fair again.

BERTRAM   My high-repented blames,
Dear sovereign, pardon to me.

---

16 *survey* sight   17 *richest* most experienced   22 *repetition* rehearsing of past
grievances   23 *The . . . dead* the particular wrongs he committed are forgotten   25 *relics* reminders   29 *hath reference to* submits himself to   32 *of season* of any one season (i.e., of steady weather)

KING   All is whole;
  Not one word more of the consumèd time.
  Let's take the instant by the forward top;   .   39
  For we are old, and on our quick'st decrees   40
  Th' inaudible and noiseless foot of time
  Steals ere we can effect them. You remember
  The daughter of this lord?

BERTRAM
  Admiringly, my liege. At first
  I stuck my choice upon her, ere my heart
  Durst make too bold a herald of my tongue;
  Where the impression of mine eye infixing,   47
  Contempt his scornful perspective did lend me,   48
  Which warped the line of every other favor,   49
  Scorned a fair color or expressed it stol'n,   50
  Extended or contracted all proportions   51
  To a most hideous object. Thence it came
  That she whom all men praised, and whom myself,   53
  Since I have lost, have loved, was in mine eye
  The dust that did offend it.

KING   Well excused;
  That thou didst love her strikes some scores away
  From the great compt. But love that comes too late,   57
  Like a remorseful pardon slowly carried,
  To the great sender turns a sour offense,   59
  Crying "That's good that's gone." Our rash faults   60
  Make trivial price of serious things we have,
  Not knowing them until we know their grave.   62
  Oft our displeasures, to ourselves unjust,   63
  Destroy our friends, and after weep their dust;   64

---

39 *forward top* forelock 47 *Where* i.e., upon Lafew's daughter 48 *perspective* distorting optical glass 49 *warped . . . favor* made the features of all other faces seem ugly 50 *color* complexion; *expressed it stol'n* declared it artificial 51–52 *Extended . . . object* stretched out or cramped together all other forms till they appeared hideous 53 *she* Helena 57 *compt* account 59 *turns . . . offense* goes sour on him 62 *Not . . . grave* not appreciating them till we've lost them for good 63 *displeasures* offenses 64 *weep their dust* mourn over their ashes

65 Our own love, waking, cries to see what's done,
66 While shameful hate sleeps out the afternoon.
    Be this sweet Helen's knell, and now forget her.
    Send forth your amorous token for fair Maudlin.
    The main consents are had, and here we'll stay
70 To see our widower's second marriage day.

COUNTESS
    Which better than the first, O dear heaven, bless,
72 Or, ere they meet, in me, O nature, cesse!

LAFEW
    Come on, my son, in whom my house's name
74 Must be digested, give a favor from you
    To sparkle in the spirits of my daughter,
    That she may quickly come.
       [Bertram gives him a ring.]
                        By my old beard
    And every hair that's on't, Helen that's dead
    Was a sweet creature; such a ring as this,
79 The last that e'er I took her leave at court,
80 I saw upon her finger.

BERTRAM   Hers it was not.

KING
    Now pray you let me see it; for mine eye,
    While I was speaking, oft was fastened to't.
       [Takes the ring.]
    This ring was mine, and when I gave it Helen
    I bade her, if her fortunes ever stood
85 Necessitied to help, that by this token
86 I would relieve her. Had you that craft to reave her
87 Of what should stead her most?

BERTRAM   My gracious sovereign,
    Howe'er it pleases you to take it so,
    The ring was never hers.

---

65 *waking* belatedly coming to its senses **66** *hate sleeps* i.e., having sated itself by destroying the friend, while love slept **72** *they* the two marriages; *meet* resemble each other; *cesse* cease **74** *digested* assimilated; *favor* love token **79** *last . . . leave* last time I took leave of her **85** *Necessitied to* in need of **86** *reave* despoil **87** *stead* aid

COUNTESS Son, on my life,
I have seen her wear it, and she reckoned it *90*
At her life's rate. *91*

LAFEW I am sure I saw her wear it.

BERTRAM
You are deceived, my lord; she never saw it.
In Florence was it from a casement thrown me,
Wrapped in a paper, which contained the name
Of her that threw it. Noble she was, and thought
I stood engaged; but when I had subscribed *96*
To mine own fortune, and informed her fully
I could not answer in that course of honor *98*
As she had made the overture, she ceased
In heavy satisfaction, and would never *100*
Receive the ring again. *101*

KING Plutus himself,
That knows the tinct and multiplying med'cine, *102*
Hath not in nature's mystery more science *103*
Than I have in this ring. 'Twas mine, 'twas Helen's,
Whoever gave it you. Then if you know *105*
That you are well acquainted with yourself,
Confess 'twas hers, and by what rough enforcement
You got it from her. She called the saints to surety *108*
That she would never put it from her finger
Unless she gave it to yourself in bed – *110*
Where you have never come – or sent it us
Upon her great disaster. *112*

BERTRAM She never saw it.

KING
Thou speak'st it falsely, as I love mine honor,
And mak'st conjectural fears to come into me

---

91 *rate* worth **96** *stood engaged* was interested (in her) **96–97** *subscribed . . . fortune* explained my situation **98** *answer . . . honor* commit myself to the same degree **100** *In heavy satisfaction* disappointed but convinced **101** *Plutus* the god of riches **102** *tinct . . . med'cine* elixir for converting base metals to gold **103** *science* knowledge **105–6** *if . . . yourself* if you know what's good for you (?) **108** *to surety* to witness **112** *Upon . . . disaster* in time of direst peril

Which I would fain shut out. If it should prove
That thou art so inhuman – 'twill not prove so,
And yet I know not – thou didst hate her deadly,
And she is dead; which nothing but to close
Her eyes myself could win me to believe,
120   More than to see this ring. Take him away.
     [Attendants arrest Bertram.]
121   My forepast proofs, howe'er the matter fall,
122   Shall tax my fears of little vanity,
123   Having vainly feared too little. Away with him;
We'll sift this matter further.

BERTRAM   If you shall prove
This ring was ever hers, you shall as easy
Prove that I husbanded her bed in Florence,
Where yet she never was.   *[Exit, guarded.]*

KING
I am wrapped in dismal thinkings.
    Enter a Gentleman.

GENTLEMAN   Gracious sovereign,
Whether I have been to blame or no, I know not:
130   Here's a petition from a Florentine,
131   Who hath for four or five removes come short
132   To tender it herself. I undertook it,
133   Vanquished thereto by the fair grace and speech
Of the poor suppliant, who by this, I know,
135   Is here attending. Her business looks in her
136   With an importing visage, and she told me,
137   In a sweet verbal brief, it did concern
Your highness with herself.

[KING] *[Reads] a letter.*   "Upon his many protestations to
140   marry me when his wife was dead, I blush to say it, he
won me. Now is the Count Rossillion a widower, his
vows are forfeited to me, and my honor's paid to him.

---

121 *forepast proofs* ills already undergone 122 *tax ... vanity* suffice to establish the legitimacy of my fears 123 *vainly* foolishly 131 *removes*
changes of residence of the court 132 *tender* offer 133 *Vanquished* per-
suaded 135 *looks* manifests itself 136 *importing* urgent 137 *verbal brief*
oral message

He stole from Florence, taking no leave, and I follow
him to his country for justice: grant it me, O king! In
you it best lies; otherwise a seducer flourishes, and a
poor maid is undone.   Diana Capilet."

LAFEW   I will buy me a son-in-law in a fair, and toll for   147
this. I'll none of him.

KING
The heavens have thought well on thee, Lafew,
To bring forth this discov'ry. Seek these suitors.   150
Go speedily, and bring again the count.
                    [Exeunt Gentleman and an Attendant.]
I am afeard the life of Helen, lady,
Was foully snatched.

COUNTESS   Now justice on the doers!
        Enter Bertram [guarded].

KING
I wonder, sir, sith wives are monsters to you,   154
And that you fly them as you swear them lordship,   155
Yet you desire to marry.
        Enter Widow, [and] Diana.
                            What woman's that?

DIANA
I am, my lord, a wretched Florentine,
Derivèd from the ancient Capilet.   158
My suit, as I do understand, you know,
And therefore know how far I may be pitied.   160

WIDOW
I am her mother, sir, whose age and honor
Both suffer under this complaint we bring,
And both shall cease, without your remedy.

KING
Come hither, count; do you know these women?

BERTRAM
My lord, I neither can nor will deny

---

147 *in a fair* (where cheap and stolen goods are sold); *toll for* get rid of **150**
suitors supplicants **154** *sith* since **155** *swear them lordship* promise them
marriage **158** *Derivèd* descended

But that I know them. Do they charge me further?

DIANA
Why do you look so strange upon your wife?

BERTRAM
She's none of mine, my lord.

DIANA   If you shall marry,
169   You give away this hand, and that is mine;
170   You give away heaven's vows, and those are mine;
     You give away myself, which is known mine;
172   For I by vow am so embodied yours
     That she which marries you must marry me –
     Either both or none.

LAFEW   Your reputation comes too short for my daughter; you are no husband for her.

BERTRAM
177   My lord, this is a fond and desp'rate creature,
178   Whom sometime I have laughed with; let your highness
     Lay a more noble thought upon mine honor
180   Than for to think that I would sink it here.

KING
181   Sir, for my thoughts, you have them ill to friend
     Till your deeds gain them. Fairer prove your honor
     Than in my thought it lies!

DIANA   Good my lord,
     Ask him upon his oath if he does think
     He had not my virginity.

KING
186   What say'st thou to her?

BERTRAM   She's impudent, my lord,
187   And was a common gamester to the camp.

DIANA
     He does me wrong, my lord. If I were so,
     He might have bought me at a common price.

---

169 *this hand* i.e., Bertram's 172 *embodied yours* united to you 177 *fond*
foolish 178 *sometime* formerly 181 *ill to friend* ill-disposed toward you
186 *impudent* immodest, wanton 187 *common gamester* whore

Do not believe him. O, behold this ring,   *190*
Whose high respect and rich validity   191
Did lack a parallel; yet for all that
He gave it to a commoner o' th' camp,
If I be one.   194
COUNTESS   He blushes, and 'tis hit.
Of six preceding ancestors, that gem,
Conferred by testament to th' sequent issue,   196
Hath it been owed and worn. This is his wife;   197
That ring's a thousand proofs.
KING   Methought you said
You saw one here in court could witness it.
DIANA
I did, my lord, but loath am to produce   *200*
So bad an instrument; his name's Parolles.
LAFEW
I saw the man today, if man he be.
KING
Find him and bring him hither.   *[Exit an Attendant.]*
BERTRAM   What of him?
He's quoted for a most perfidious slave,   204
With all the spots o' th' world taxed and deboshed,   205
Whose nature sickens but to speak a truth.
Am I or that or this for what he'll utter,
That will speak anything?
KING   She hath that ring of yours.
BERTRAM
I think she has. Certain it is I liked her,
And boarded her i' th' wanton way of youth.   *210*
She knew her distance and did angle for me,
Madding my eagerness with her restraint –   212
As all impediments in fancy's course   213
Are motives of more fancy – and in fine   214

---

191 *respect* worth; *validity* value 194 *'tis hit* the charge is proved 196 *se-*
quent issue next generation 197 *owed* owned 204 *quoted* noted 205
taxed and deboshed charged with debauchery 210 *boarded* accosted 212
Madding spurring 213 *in fancy's course* in amorous pursuit 214 *fancy*
erotic fantasies; *in fine* at length

215   Her infinite cunning with her modern grace
216   Subdued me to her rate. She got the ring,
        And I had that which any inferior might
        At market price have bought.

DIANA   I must be patient.
        You that have turned off a first so noble wife
220   May justly diet me. I pray you yet –
        Since you lack virtue, I will lose a husband –
        Send for your ring, I will return it home,
        And give me mine again.

BERTRAM   I have it not.

KING
        What ring was yours, I pray you?

DIANA   Sir, much like
        The same upon your finger.

KING
        Know you this ring? This ring was his of late.

DIANA
        And this was it I gave him, being abed.

KING
        The story then goes false, you threw it him
        Out of a casement?

DIANA   I have spoke the truth.
        Enter Parolles.

BERTRAM
230   My lord, I do confess the ring was hers.

KING
231   You boggle shrewdly; every feather starts you.
        Is this the man you speak of?

DIANA   Ay, my lord.

KING
        Tell me, sirrah – but tell me true, I charge you,
        Not fearing the displeasure of your master,

---

215 *modern* commonplace   216 *Subdued . . . rate* made me accept her terms
220 *diet me* i.e., pay me my wages and send me packing   231 *boggle
shrewdly* shy nervously; *starts* startles

Which, on your just proceeding, I'll keep off —   235
By him and by this woman here what know you?   236

PAROLLES   So please your majesty, my master hath been
    an honorable gentleman. Tricks he hath had in him,
    which gentlemen have.

KING   Come, come, to th' purpose. Did he love this   240
    woman?

PAROLLES   Faith, sir, he did love her; but how?

KING   How, I pray you?

PAROLLES   He did love her, sir, as a gentleman loves a   244
    woman.

KING   How is that?

PAROLLES   He loved her, sir, and loved her not.   247

KING   As thou art a knave, and no knave. What an
    equivocal companion is this!   249

PAROLLES   I am a poor man, and at your majesty's com-   250
    mand.

LAFEW   He's a good drum, my lord, but a naughty orator.   252

DIANA   Do you know he promised me marriage?

PAROLLES   Faith, I know more than I'll speak.

KING   But wilt thou not speak all thou know'st?

PAROLLES   Yes, so please your majesty. I did go between
    them as I said; but more than that, he loved her — for
    indeed he was mad for her, and talked of Satan and of
    Limbo and of Furies and I know not what. Yet I was in   259
    that credit with them at that time that I knew of their   260
    going to bed, and of other motions, as promising her   261
    marriage, and things which would derive me ill will to   262
    speak of; therefore I will not speak what I know.

KING   Thou hast spoken all already, unless thou canst say
    they are married; but thou art too fine in thy evidence;   265
    therefore stand aside.

---

235 *on . . . proceeding* if you tell the truth   236 *By* concerning   244–45 *a
woman* (1) sexual conquest, (2) a non-noble woman   247 *He loved . . . not*
he pursued her sexually but had no other interest in her   249 *companion* rascal   252 *drum* drummer; *naughty* worthless   259–60 *in . . . them* in their
confidence   261 *motions* proposals   262 *derive* gain   265 *fine* subtle

This ring you say was yours?

DIANA   Ay, my good lord.

KING

Where did you buy it? or who gave it you?

DIANA

It was not given me, nor I did not buy it.

KING

270 Who lent it you?

DIANA   It was not lent me neither.

KING

Where did you find it then?

DIANA   I found it not.

KING

If it were yours by none of all these ways,
How could you give it him?

DIANA   I never gave it him.

LAFEW   This woman's an easy glove, my lord; she goes off
and on at pleasure.

KING

This ring was mine; I gave it his first wife.

DIANA

It might be yours or hers for aught I know.

KING

Take her away, I do not like her now;
To prison with her, and away with him.

280 Unless thou tell'st me where thou hadst this ring,
Thou diest within this hour.

DIANA   I'll never tell you.

KING

282 Take her away.

DIANA   I'll put in bail, my liege.

KING

283 I think thee now some common customer.

DIANA

284 By Jove, if ever I knew man, 'twas you.

---

282 *put in bail* make good on my story   **283** *customer* prostitute   **284** *knew*
i.e., sexually

KING
   Wherefore hast thou accused him all this while?

DIANA
   Because he's guilty, and he is not guilty.
   He knows I am no maid, and he'll swear to't;
   I'll swear I am a maid and he knows not.
   Great king, I am no strumpet, by my life;
   I am either maid, or else this old man's wife.   290
     [Points to Lafew.]

KING
   She does abuse our ears; to prison with her!

DIANA
   Good mother, fetch my bail. Stay, royal sir,
                      [Exit Widow.]
   The jeweler that owes the ring is sent for,   293
   And he shall surety me. But for this lord,   294
   Who hath abused me, as he knows himself,
   Though yet he never harmed me, here I quit him.   296
   He knows himself my bed he hath defiled,
   And at that time he got his wife with child.
   Dead though she be, she feels her young one kick.
   So there's my riddle: one that's dead is quick –   300
   And now behold the meaning.   301
     Enter Helena and Widow.

KING   Is there no exorcist
   Beguiles the truer office of mine eyes?   302
   Is't real that I see?

HELENA   No, my good lord,
   'Tis but the shadow of a wife you see,
   The name and not the thing.

BERTRAM   Both, both; O, pardon!

HELENA
   O my good lord, when I was like this maid   306

---

293 *owes* owns   294 *surety me* be my security   296 *quit* acquit, release   300 *quick* alive (with pun on *with child*)   301 *exorcist* magician   302 *Beguiles . . . office* deceives the true vision   306 *like this maid* disguised as her, in her place

I found you wondrous kind. There is your ring,
And look you, here's your letter. This it says:
"When from my finger you can get this ring,
310   And are by me with child," etc. This is done.
Will you be mine, now you are doubly won?

BERTRAM
If she, my liege, can make me know this clearly,
I'll love her dearly – ever, ever dearly.

HELENA
If it appear not plain, and prove untrue,
Deadly divorce step between me and you.
O my dear mother, do I see you living?

LAFEW
Mine eyes smell onions; I shall weep anon.
   [To Parolles]
Good Tom Drum, lend me a handkercher. So, I thank
thee. Wait on me home; I'll make sport with thee. Let
320   thy curtsies alone; they are scurvy ones.

KING
Let us from point to point this story know,
322   To make the even truth in pleasure flow.
   [To Diana]
If thou beest yet a fresh uncroppèd flower,
Choose thou thy husband, and I'll pay thy dower;
For I can guess that by thy honest aid
Thou kept'st a wife herself, thyself a maid.
Of that and all the progress more and less
328   Resolvedly more leisure shall express.
329   All yet seems well, and if it end so meet,
330   The bitter past, more welcome is the sweet.   *Flourish.*

[EPILOGUE]

[KING]
The king's a beggar, now the play is done.
All is well ended if this suit be won,

---

320 *curtsies* reverences **322** *even* exact **328** *Resolvedly* with full explanation
329 *meet* fittingly

That you express content; which we will pay   333
With strife to please you, day exceeding day.   334
Ours be your patience then, and yours our parts;   335
Your gentle hands lend us, and take our hearts.

Exeunt omnes.

---

333 *express content* i.e., by applause   334 *strife* effort   335 *Ours . . . parts* we
will become the audience (to your applause) while you become the actors (by
applauding)

The distinguished Pelican Shakespeare series, newly revised
to be the premier choice for students, professors, and
general readers well into the 21st century

All's Well That Ends Well
ISBN 0-14-071460-X

Antony and Cleopatra
ISBN 0-14-071452-9

As You Like It
ISBN 0-14-071471-5

The Comedy of Errors
ISBN 0-14-071474-X

Coriolanus
ISBN 0-14-071473-1

Cymbeline
ISBN 0-14-071472-3

Hamlet
ISBN 0-14-071454-5

Henry IV, Part I
ISBN 0-14-071456-1

Henry IV, Part 2
ISBN 0-14-071457-X

Henry V
ISBN 0-14-071458-8

Henry VI, Part 1
ISBN 0-14-071465-0

Henry VI, Part 2
ISBN 0-14-071466-9

Henry VI, Part 3
ISBN 0-14-071467-7

Henry VIII
ISBN 0-14-071475-8

Julius Caesar
ISBN 0-14-071468-5

King John
ISBN 0-14-071459-6

King Lear
ISBN 0-14-071476-6

*King Lear
(The Quarto and Folio Texts)*
ISBN 0-14-071490-1

Love's Labor's Lost
ISBN 0-14-071477-4

Macbeth
ISBN 0-14-071478-2

Measure for Measure
ISBN 0-14-071479-0

The Merchant of Venice
ISBN 0-14-071462-6

The Merry Wives of Windsor
ISBN 0-14-071464-2

A Midsummer Night's Dream
ISBN 0-14-071455-3

Much Ado About Nothing
ISBN 0-14-071480-4

The Narrative Poems
ISBN 0-14-071481-2

Othello
ISBN 0-14-071463-4

Pericles
ISBN 0-14-071469-3

Richard II
ISBN 0-14-071482-0

Richard III
ISBN 0-14-071483-9

Romeo and Juliet
ISBN 0-14-071484-7

The Sonnets
ISBN 0-14-071453-7

The Taming of the Shrew
ISBN 0-14-071451-0

The Tempest
ISBN 0-14-071485-5

Timon of Athens
ISBN 0-14-071487-1

Titus Andronicus
ISBN 0-14-071491-X

Troilus and Cressida
ISBN 0-14-071486-3

Twelfth Night
ISBN 0-14-071489-8

The Two Gentlemen of Verona
ISBN 0-14-071461-8

The Winter's Tale
ISBN 0-14-071488-X

FOR THE BEST IN PAPERBACKS, LOOK FOR THE

In every corner of the world, on every subject under the sun, Penguin represents quality and variety—the very best in publishing today.

For complete information about books available from Penguin—including Puffins, Penguin Classics, and Compass—and how to order them, write to us at the appropriate address below. Please note that for copyright reasons the selection of books varies from country to country.

In the United Kingdom: Please write to *Dept. EP, Penguin Books Ltd, Bath Road, Harmondsworth, West Drayton, Middlesex UB7 0DA.*

In the United States: Please write to *Penguin Putnam Inc., P.O. Box 12289 Dept. B, Newark, New Jersey 07101-5289* or call 1-800-788-6262.

In Canada: Please write to *Penguin Books Canada Ltd, 10 Alcorn Avenue, Suite 300, Toronto, Ontario M4V 3B2.*

In Australia: Please write to *Penguin Books Australia Ltd, P.O. Box 257, Ringwood, Victoria 3134.*

In New Zealand: Please write to *Penguin Books (NZ) Ltd, Private Bag 102902, North Shore Mail Centre, Auckland 10.*

In India: Please write to *Penguin Books India Pvt Ltd, 11 Panchsheel Shopping Centre, Panchsheel Park, New Delhi 110 017.*

In the Netherlands: Please write to *Penguin Books Netherlands bv, Postbus 3507, NL-1001 AH Amsterdam.*

In Germany: Please write to *Penguin Books Deutschland GmbH, Metzlerstrasse 26, 60594 Frankfurt am Main.*

In Spain: Please write to *Penguin Books S. A., Bravo Murillo 19, 1° B, 28015 Madrid.*

In Italy: Please write to *Penguin Italia s.r.l., Via Benedetto Croce 2, 20094 Corsico, Milano.*

In France: Please write to *Penguin France, Le Carré Wilson, 62 rue Benjamin Baillaud, 31500 Toulouse.*

In Japan: Please write to *Penguin Books Japan Ltd, Kaneko Building, 2-3-25 Koraku, Bunkyo-Ku, Tokyo 112.*

In South Africa: Please write to *Penguin Books South Africa (Pty) Ltd, Private Bag X14, Parkview, 2122 Johannesburg.*